ANOTHER RESCUE MISSION

Reviving the mission that once saved the United Kingdom (UK)

By

Ayo Ogunbuyide

Endorsed by

Agu Irukwu

Published by New Generation Publishing in 2024

Copyright © Ayo Ogunbuyide 2024

First Edition

The author asserts the moral right under the Copyright, Designs and Patents Act 1988 to be identified as the author of this work.

All Rights reserved. No part of this publication may be reproduced, stored in a retrieval system or transmitted, in any form or by any means without the prior consent of the author, nor be otherwise circulated in any form of binding or cover other than that which it is published and without a similar condition being imposed on the subsequent purchaser.

Paperback ISBN: 978-1-83563-068-6
Hardback ISBN: 978-1-83563-069-3

www.newgeneration-publishing.com

New Generation Publishing

TABLE OF CONTENTS

Acknowledgement vi
Foreword viii
Endorsement ix
Introduction xi
Preface xiii
Chapter 1 The darkness of the UK in the 19th century 1
   1.1 Reasons behind 19th Century high crime rate 2
   1.2 Is another Industrial Revolution around the corner? 3
   1.3 Beyond prescribed interventions 5
   1.4 The new force and a unique mark of difference 6

Chapter 2 Light in the darkness 12
   2.1 How court mission emerged 12
   2.2 The work began to grow 15
   2.3 Making life worth living 16
   2.4 Embraced by law 17
   2.5 A typical day in court for the missionaries 19
   2.6 The end of LPCM 23

Chapter 3 19th century faith pioneers of change 24
   3.1 The man, Frederic Rainer 24
   3.2 Strength of the 1st rescue mission 27
   3.3 His mentorship connection 28
   3.4 The case for youth involvement 29

3.5 Fifty years of uncommon impact............................ 30

3.6 Rainer was unstoppable.. 31

3.7 Sir Robert Peel, his legacy of peace in England and Ireland 31

3.8 Amazing discovery... 32

Chapter 4 Rebuilding the broken walls of society 36

4.1 The government makes the same suggestion as court missionaries... 36

4.2 Remodeling homes, reconciling couples............... 38

4.3 Testimonies and strategies 40

4.4 Averting the shipwreck of young lives.................. 41

4.5 Personal experience.. 42

4.6 Boys' Shelter Home, Camberwell.......................... 44

4.7 From failed home to a fulfilled life 44

4.8 They are no longer fatherless robbers 46

4.9 Court missionaries' work with women and girls... 46

4.10 Found real life after suicide attempt.................... 47

4.11 All she needed was a chance................................ 47

PART 2

Chapter 5 The scourge is here again............................50

5.1 The 21st century social plague 51

5.2 Drug use 51

5.3 Suggested cause of drug use.................................. 52

5.4 Gaps within government provisions that are contributing to the surge in drug use............................ 53

5.5 Phase two of Professor Dame Carol Black's report 54

5.6 Diverting more offenders into treatment and recovery services 54

5.7 The improvement of prisoners treatment experience in and out of prison 55

5.8 Employment support 55

5.9 Housing 56

Chapter 6 The old way the major way out 58

6.1 Central government response 59

6.2 Breaking the drug chain supply 60

6.3 Delivering a world-class treatment and recovery system 60

6.4 Achieve generational shift in demand for drugs ... 61

6.5 Analysis of this response 63

Chapter 7 Emerging rescue mission 66

7.1 Viable partnership examples 69

7.2 Examples of a few existing Christian charities 72

Chapter 8 Starting a new community organisation? 76

Chapter 9 79

The unique love story 79

References 81

Acknowledgement

I want to express my profound gratitude to God Almighty for giving me the grace to write this book. He saw me through the three years of relentless research. I thank Him for the strength, energy, and outcomes of all my endeavors.

I want to thank my amazing wife Oluwaseun for her tremendous support. I gave up writing this book in 2022 December when I lost a huge chunk of data and findings I had compiled for over six months. I woke up one morning and they were gone from my laptop! However, she stopped at nothing to encourage me to keep writing. If not for her, I would have given up writing this book completely.

I extend my love to my two lovely children for the enthusiasm and support they show for all I do. Their excitement about this book is almost more than mine. I love you, Mofi and Sam!

A big thank you to Felix and Esther Awosope for proofreading this book. I love you both immensely.

To Reverend Canon 'Yemi Adedeji, you make leadership attractive, and I want to thank you for the privilege you have given me to learn from you.

To Mark North, the CEO of Freedom Community Project. I deeply appreciate you for the time, support, and advice you provided on this project. Thank you, Mark!

Finally, to Pastor Agu Irukwu, what can I say? Your leadership approach has set a standard for the upcoming generation of leaders. Your passion for underserved communities, dedication to persecuted churches globally and your heart for people is contagious and inspiring. Taking time out of your extremely busy schedule to support the writing of this book and giving it your endorsement means a lot to me. Thank you, a million times.

> I dedicate this book to the vulnerable and underserved communities in the United Kingdom. May the light of hope shine on you.

Foreword

Another Rescue Mission is indeed a worthwhile book to read for a much-needed Church Rescue Mission.
Our world today is filled with offenders that the Criminal Justice System and the Society find easy to cancel and put away with hope that incarceration will be the solution.

This book will provoke the mind of any reader and will surely help connect the history of probation service to our present day need and hopefully help the church and the society to navigate the future.

The Rev'd Canon Yemi Adedeji
Consultant | Coach | Speaker | Author | Minister
yemiadedeji.com

"In Another Rescue Mission, Ayo Ogunbuyide highlights historical examples of past British Christian Mission. Showing how the British Court system was changed by passionate Christians seeking an approach that transformed people rather than just punished them. Ayo shows the impact of these missions, how they played a part in social transformation. Ayo challenges the Church and Christian Missions to engage in partnerships with Local and National government to see the current society transformed."

Mark North
Chief Executive Officer
Freedom Community Project

Endorsement

Another Rescue Mission is a very timely addition to the discussions taking place now about the criminal justice system. Particularly within the probation system. This well researched and superbly written book is certainly part of the rescue mission to save a system that was once the envy of other nations but is sadly today barely coping and in certain instances has probably broken down.

When put together the statistics paint a picture of a system that is no longer achieving the objectives and is desperately in need of change. It is important to highlight the amazing work that is being done by probation officers all around the country within the constraints of a system that is in need of an overhaul. This thrust of the book is to return to a system that worked. That system harnessed the resources available in the Church with results to show for it. Without sounding alarmist, we as a nation are facing a crisis in our criminal justice system, overcrowded prisons, a creaking process in our courts, overstretched police officer, and other parts that are not functioning how they are supposed to function.

A part of the solution must surely be as the book urges, a collaboration between the government and faith groups. This collaboration with the church has worked in the past and there is no reason why it should not work again. The challenge from this book to all the parties involved, the government at various levels, the church (and other faith groups), the enforcement agencies and the politicians are to make this happen. You perceive in Ayo's writing his grasp of the urgency of this issue. It really is time for another rescue mission.

I would commend this book to all who desire to see a healthy criminal justice system in our nation and of course a thriving society for all especially the underserved and marginalised.

Agu Irukwu
Senior Pastor
Jesus House for all the Nations
Brent Cross, London

Introduction

It is important to note that most of the public service provisions we enjoy now in the United Kingdom are deeply rooted in Christianity.

Another Rescue Mission is the outcome of my three-year research into the history of the UK probation service. Reliable and verifiable data show historic connection between the UK Probation system and the Church of England. Especially the input of Frederic Rainer, a local printer from Hertfordshire who was a committed member of the Church of England Temperance Society (CETS). In addition to this, you'll find the fascinating story of Sir Robert Peel, the man behind the establishment of the Metropolitan Police in 1829. He was a two-time Home Secretary, two-time Prime Minister of England and a one-time Chief Secretary of Ireland.

Although they are known as probation officers today, in the mid-19th Century and early 20th Century they were called police court missionaries. The impact of their work was so effective that after three decades they were adopted into law through the 1907 Probation of Offenders Act. The high wave of alcohol-related crime that ravaged England in the 19th Century defiled many interventions which, largely, was the imprisonment of those who committed drink-related offences. However, the emergence of the work of the police court missionaries brought radical change to the narrative.

The Home Secretary at the time, Sir William Joynson-Hicks, had this to say about the extraordinary result of the police court missionaries:

"I do not know what we should do without the Mission work, or how we could carry on the remedial side of the Police Court without it." He went on further to say: "The Magistrates, instead of sending offenders to prison, hand many of them over to the missionaries to be visited, looked after, and kept in touch with, and see, as far as it is humanly possible, that they have a chance to get back on the right lines again."

Another Rescue Mission is a call back to the system that has been proven to work. Why? The 21st Century United Kingdom has been plagued, once again, with drug addiction. As of 2019, the UK illicit drug market was worth a yearly amount of £9.4 billion.

In this book, you'll find the summary of Professor Dame Carol Black's findings. She was commissioned by the UK government in 2019 to carry out an independent review of drug addiction and the current government provisions used to tackle it. She declared the current government provisions to tackle drug addiction as "inadequate." Coincidentally, most of her recommendations were the same as the recommendations and actions of the 19th century police court missionaries.

One thing remains clear, there is an urgent need for another rescue mission. The time is now. The Church must rise like the 19th century Church did. A healthy collaboration must transpire between the government and the Church for another mission to rescue.

Preface

It took me three years to research the facts and data that informed the writing of this book. Not because the topic is that complex, but I struggled with relevant data because they were difficult to find.

According to Cassady (2001) *"Little is written about the man who is said to have taken that first step, and few beyond the areas of probation know of his work."* It was a struggle for me to gather relevant evidence around the impact and contribution of the Church to the development of the UK probation service especially about, Frederic Rainer who championed this move.

Thankfully, during my research, I eventually came across the minutes of meetings and annual reports by the CETS; some of which dated back to over 100 years ago. It is amazing that this is still available. It is also commendable that the Nottingham Gallery of Justice now has the Rainer Foundation Archive.

The lesson here is this: past social efforts of the Christian faith may have been undermined due to lack of records. Churches and Christian faith organisations must begin to document and archive their community development work for posterity's sake.

I must state that this book is not just focused on probation or criminal justice. I am just using the probation service and the transformation of the UK's penal culture as an example of one, out of many, contributions of the Christian faith to social transformation and development. **'Another Rescue**

Mission' Is a blueprint for emerging 'Social Reformers'. The world is in dire need of one.

This book is divided into two sessions. The first four chapters gives an insight into the history of UK Probation and the immense part played by the Police Court Missionaries in making it a reality. It also talks about Frederic Rainer and Sir Rebert Peel, men whose faith impacted the creation of the UK Probation system and the introduction of the metropolitan police respectively.

The final part highlights independent reviews with recommendations that points the nation back to similar interventions of over a hundred years ago. These recommendations are similar to the discoveries which the Police Court Missionaries executed in the 19th Century, and it became a blueprint. It appears we are back to where we used to be. The questions are; will the recommendations of Professor Dame Carol Black be executed? Will the Christian faith rise to the rescue of society again? Will the collaboration be given another chance?

Reliable secondary research was adopted when making relevant findings for this book. The CETS annual report, the memoir, titled *Inasmuch,* of the CETS one-time secretary Hasloch J. Porter, as well as other reliable and verifiable online sources, and my personal experience in community work all aided the writing of this book. Qualitative and quantitative research was also used in analyzing specific findings to aid understanding.

Ayo Ogunbuyide

Chapter 1
The darkness of the UK in the 19th century

"Once a person got into trouble through drink or other cause, there seems no hope for him. Offence after offence and sentence after sentence appeared to be the inevitable lot for him or her whose foot had once slipped. Can nothing be done to stop this downward career? I hope that some practical work could (sic) be organised in the police courts, and I enclose five shillings that a fund may be started so that an agent may be appointed to attend the police courts to help the prisoners." (A fraction of Frederic Rainer's letter to the Church of England Temperance Society in 1875).

These lines were picked from a letter written by a gentleman called Frederic Rainer in 1875, which was addressed to the leadership of the Church of England Temperance Society, of which he was a committed member. As of the time he wrote this letter, alcohol-related offences and alcohol addiction was wrecking lives. According to Rainer, the lives of the people affected were on a "downward slope."

Therefore, he wrote this letter and accompanied with it was a donation of five shillings. This donation of five shillings was to go towards the redemption of these lives. This was the first financial aid into the project that eventually evolved into what we now refer to as the United Kingdom probation system. The United Kingdom probation system was the result of a burning passion and desire in the heart of the Hertfordshire printer, Frederic Rainer, from the Church of England, to see the reclamation of alcohol-related offenders. In other words, the ideology, and the initial start-up grant for what is known today as the UK probation service came from a Christian through his Church.

The 18th century United Kingdom was plagued with so much criminal activity that was directly, or indirectly, linked to high-level alcohol addiction and substance misuse. History has recorded that this period saw the great rise of lawlessness and immorality. McWilliams (1983) explained the level of lawlessness experienced in the nation. He recorded that the period between 1860 and 1876 experienced an incredible wave of alcohol-related offences in the country and the use of imprisonment to address these offences yielded very little results. Rev. G.P. Merrick, who was actively involved in the work of the court missionaries, stated that three quarters of prison cells were loaded with female alcohol-related offenders.

1.1 Reasons behind 19th Century high crime rate

It is important to note that until 1829 when Sir Robert Peel was successful in pushing through the proposal for the Metropolitan Police Act, England had no structured police force. Law enforcement had experienced a lot of evolution and transition before then. However, Sir Robert Peel was instrumental in the introduction of the 1829 London Metropolitan Police Act. This eventually became a footprint to the nationwide establishment of structured policing. Until the creation of the London Metropolitan police, crime was prevalent across the country. Sir Robert Peel saw the widespread criminal activity in England as a threat to national stability (parliament.uk, 2023). He was another pioneer whose work brought about a significant change in the history of the establishment of law and order in England and Ireland. It is noteworthy that Sir Robert Peel was a committed Christian. However, I'll give further details about this in chapter 3.

Some other historic accounts linked the high wave of alcohol-related offences to the 19th century Industrial Revolution. The 19th century Industrial Revolution refers to the period of diversion from the use of human beings to the use of machinery in the workplace, particularly in factories. Hand production was gradually being replaced with machine manufacturing. The Industrial Revolution, in the UK, started around 1760 and lasted until around the 1820's to the 1840's. Although at the initial stage the industrial revolution was challenging, eventually it led to great output and a prosperous economy. This was because workers who were engaged in hand production lost their jobs, and many were unable to find any other work because their skills were no longer seen as needed in the job market. This eventually led to widespread hunger and poverty. Inevitably, several of those impacted turned to crime to survive and to alcohol addiction as coping mechanism.

1.2 Is another Industrial Revolution around the corner?

In July 2023, I was watching the news and it had been reported that Hollywood actors were protesting the use of artificial intelligence (AI) to capture and use their likeness without their permission. This occurred a few weeks after Hollywood writers went on strike in reaction to artificial intelligence being used to write screenplays. According to the news, the last time Hollywood protested was in 1960.

My reflection here is simple. Are we getting close to another Industrial Revolution with the current advancement in technology and the emergence of artificial intelligence? The use of ChatGPT in executing secretarial and administrative tasks is gradually becoming notable.

In cities across England, we've already seen the implementation of machines and robots who conveniently do light shopping deliveries. Many years ago, you would need to physically go to your bank or building society in order to deposit money, but nowadays a lot of transactions can be done online. Even when you go to banks you can easily deposit through a cash machine. Self-service machines in shops are frequently used to pay for light grocery shopping, and it won't be surprising if in few years similar machines are produced for huge shopping trips. High-street shopping is gradually being relegated because of the ease of online shopping. I have friends who have not been to the high street or their own town center for a year! Amazon has made online shopping easier and more attractive to people.

Technical advancement is putting jobs at risk. Yet, I believe we are still going to witness more innovations in technology.

Factors such as the frequent slash of government budget across countries, the effects of the Covid-19 pandemic on socio-economic life, the cost-of-living crisis, the increase in energy costs and tariffs etc, are undeniably and aggressively present and are continuously threatening the economic wellbeing of many countries. The impact that this has had on citizens is enormous.

It is, therefore, important for governments across board to brace up and ensure that people don't fall through the cracks. We must be intentional in avoiding another crime and addiction wave like the one that arose because of the 19th ccentury Industrial Revolution. I have used latter chapters of this book to address the ongoing surge in addiction and crime in the United Kingdom and I believe this is applicable to many countries. We are almost back at the same point we found ourselves in almost two centuries ago. All hands must be on deck, we must not ignore the signs. This is why I believe this book is timely.

1.3 Beyond prescribed interventions

The high wave of alcohol-related offences in the country appeared to have gone beyond remedy. Then in 1839, precisely nine years after Sir Robert Peel left office as Home Secretary, the 1839 Metropolitan Police Act was introduced. One power, among many others, bestowed upon the police through this law, was the power to jail "drunkards guilty of riotous or indecent behaviour." (Jennings, 2012) Police arrests and legal prosecution became the order of the day for "drunkards" who were caught behaving indecently in public. In turn, this scared a lot of people who were worried about being arrested even if they weren't drinking. People continued to partake in their drinking habit, but now with the added fear of being caught.

Interestingly, it is on record that there was a reduction in the number of alcohol-related crime cases that went to court by the middle of the 19th century. Having said that, alcohol-related crime and offences still accounted for most of the cases brought before the courts. For example, in 1885, the prosecution of drunkenness accounted for 26,614 charges in the metropolis alone (Porter, 1927). Obviously, people's lives continued a downward slope due to uncontrolled use of alcohol. It was obvious that the law did not stop people from drinking, but people only avoided arrest by behaving themselves in public.

As stated above, people became afraid of being arrested. However, they knew that the police only arrested those who constituted nuisance in public, therefore, people mastered the act of behaving themselves publicly, but, privately, alcohol addiction continued to wreck lives.

One unforeseen consequence of using jail time to control alcohol-related offences, was that those who were jailed often came out to commit worse crimes than they did before they went in. Porter (1927) stated that in nine out of ten cases, offenders who were sentenced to jail came out of jail worse than they went in. This was the start of recycling offenders within the criminal justice system. First time offenders who went to jail for being drunk, came out with a much more extensive knowledge of crime because they met and mingled with people who indulged in worse crimes. Their association with such people in prison had negative and devastating effects on their lives, and on the society into which they were released after their sentence.

Re-offending continued to have grievous consequences on the socio-economic life of the country. It put a lot of pressure on public spending because a lot of funds went towards the care and maintenance of the growing number of inmates in various prisons across the UK.

1.4 The new force and a unique mark of difference

"Official buttons could only frighten away; the power of a spiritual agency was needed to get at the back of offences, to reach the hearts of offenders." (Porter, 1927)

Then, in 1876, the court missionaries emerged. With this development came a different approach as well as outstanding results and outcomes. Their approach eventually became an adopted blueprint for the nation. With them came a deviation from the existing framework of prison-time and fines as a punishment for offenders. They offered something different.

Criminology experts said that the court missionaries moved away from the classical approach and switched towards a positivist approach to the penal system. The classical approach towards the penal system sees offending as a choice that an individual makes, and such choices must be followed by severe legal consequences. This may take the form of tough legal measures such as imprisonment or fines.

Whereas criminologists believed that court missionaries practiced a positivist approach towards the penal system. This approach believes that offending is the result of tough economic and social circumstances or conditions (Wiener, 1990). Court missionaries believed the best way to help those who were taken to court was to investigate the reasons behind the crimes that were committed and provide relevant solutions to remove those reasons.

Court missionaries concerned themselves with the removal of the reasons behind crime. They were interested in the whys, such as "why did you commit the crime?" which they often got to understand through their uncommon friendly approach. The system often rejected offenders by locking them away behind bars, but the Church embraced them. The ethics behind the police court missionaries' befriending those charged to court often earned them the trust and confidence of offenders, which in turn meant that offenders found it easy to be open with court missionaries.

Their work ethic was different. The court missionaries and their work often stuck to the ethics of "advise, assist and befriend." (Jarvis, 1972)

When they interacted with offenders, they did't see criminals, the court missionaries saw people through the lens of hope, potential, and possibility. This was because of the ethics of their Christian faith. The Holy Bible motivated the gesture of the court missionaries:

"So, from now on, we refuse to evaluate people merely by their outward appearances." 2 Corinthians 5:16a (The Passion Translation)

The court missionaries saw the offenders this exact same way, they did't judge offenders based on their outward appearance, or on whatever it was they may have done. The court missionaries annual report from 1903 explains this better:

"As the editor of their published annual report suggested in 1903, to 'separate the victim from the cause' was to practice 'something of the Divine Compassion" (Porter, 1927)

Divine compassion is one of the basic Christian ethics that the Bible teaches. The court missionaries practiced it, and their results changed the nation. Court missionaries separated the victims from the crimes they committed. They saw value in people, they saw people who had missed the right path in life and the court missionaries believed that with some help, they could reclaim and restore the offenders. At the start of this chapter, we read this quote from Frederic Rainer's letter:

"Offence after offence and sentence after sentence appeared to be the inevitable lot for him or her whose foot had once slipped. Can nothing be done to stop this downward career?" (Porter, 1927)

He referred to the offenders as people whose feet once slipped, and that hope was possible with a little help. Through divine and Christ-like compassion, the court missionaries changed the dynamics of criminal justice in

England. This compassion embraced those that the system had previously rejected.

The results of the court missionaries astounded the entire system. Professionals began to express their utmost surprise at the outcomes and achievements of the court missionaries. Their outcomes on those charged before the court was unimaginable.

In June 1925, the Chief Constable of Wigan made this remark about the court missionaries:

"I have been asked to give my opinion of the C.E.T.S. Police Court Mission, and I do so with very great pleasure. I am probably in a better position than most people to testify as to the efficacy of their charitable work. The helpful counsels, interminable patience and practical assistance of their Missionaries in the Police Court is absolutely invaluable, and I know from practical experience that they have been the means of salvation to many unfortunate."

Porter (1927) gave a few instances where court missionaries were able to rescue offenders from a prison sentence and instead helped them achieve far better outcomes. I will round out this chapter by sharing some of those examples.

Example 1

A lady aged 49 with over ten convictions of drunkenness had her life totally turned around for the better.

A female court missionary was working with her. This female court missionary wouldn't' give up on this lady despite her repeated sentences for drink-related offences. Each time she would get released from prison, the female court missionary met with her, prayed for her and told her affirmatively "I will never give up praying for you, and trying to help you."

The straw that broke the camel's back was the last time the offender came out of prison. In the room where the missionary met with the offender after being released, hung a picture of Jesus Christ on the cross. The missionary met with the offender and prayed for her. As usual, the offender asked "Why ever do you go on praying for me, though I'm not worth it?" The missionary responded "Well, He thought you were worth dying for, dear." She said this pointing to the picture of Jesus on the cross. The lady offender broke down in tears and that was the beginning of her journey to totally turning around and creating a new life. Not only did she abstain from drinking and getting into crime, she became a cleaner in a hospital (Porter, 1927).

Example 2

A man had been arrested and charged to court for vagrancy. The word *vagrant* refers anyone who has no fixed address, wanders aimlessly with no means of income, and sometimes uses drugs or excessive alcohol. Vagrancy was punishable by law in the United Kingdom throughout the 19th century.

Before the introduction of court missionaries, he would have been sentenced to prison. However, the court asked a court missionary to work with the offender and make some inquiries. Apparently, the offender had gone out in search of employment and gotten none. He got back home and found his wife and child crying because they had not eaten and there was nothing in the house for the family to eat. He had no other choice but to resort to begging. He got arrested while begging and charged to court. These were the findings of the court missionary and based on these findings, the offender was discharged. Not only that, but the immediate needs of the family, such as food, were supplied by the court missionary and some work was found for the man. Normally, without the involvement of the court missionary, this poor man would have earned a prison sentence (Moore, 1902).

Chapter 2
Light in the darkness

"The ordinary drunkard cares little about fines, or mild terms of imprisonment. It is not in human nature that a man, with his favourite bottle before him, will refrain from emptying it for fear of such consequences." (Plowden, 1903)

Alfred Plowman was a barrister and magistrate at the Metropolitan Police Magistrates Court on Marlborough Street. He wasn't a novice of the United Kingdom criminal justice system, he was an active player. He spoke from a place of understanding what was going on with the deployment of the penal system to address alcohol addiction and its failures.

He attested to the fact that no one who was addicted to alcohol would refrain from their drinking habit because of fines or jail-time.

This chapter tells the story of how the court missionaries emerged.

2.1 How court mission emerged

In May of 1862, Rev. Dr Close — who happened to be the Dean of Carlisle — formed the Church of England Total Abstinence Society, and Reverend (afterwards Canon) H.J Ellison emerged as the Chairman. At the time of this, Rev Ellison was the vicar of Windsor. 13 years later, this group was reconstituted and became the Church of England

Temperance Society (CETS). The function of CETS was to advocate for abstinence from alcohol.

Primarily, their duty was to visit public places like pubs, cabstands etc., and encourage people to sign an abstinence pledge. An abstinence pledge was simply the act of someone who was addicted to alcohol signing their name saying that they won't indulge in the act anymore. Members of the CETS would then follow up on the pledge and those who signed it to ensure that they were abiding by their commitment. These actions defined their activity until 1876.

In 1875, a local Hertfordshire printer began to develop a feeling of regret for those whose lives were sinking in the devastating and horrific claws of alcohol and jail-time. A lot more about Frederic Rainer will be discussed in Chapter 3. The government's intervention of fines and imprisonment had obviously not done a lot to improve the lives of the victims of alcohol. Fortunately, Frederic Rainer was a mentee of Reverend Ellison. Historical records suggest that Reverend Ellison introduced Frederic Rainer to the work of CETS and encouraged Rainer to be actively involved in it.

At this time, Rainer wrote to Reverend Ellison. This letter eventually went on to form the roots of the redemption of thousands of people whose lives were going down the drain because of alcohol addiction. This letter eventually reformed the United Kingdom criminal justice system, shaped probation and the expression of social work to a high degree.

"Once a person got into trouble through drink or other cause, there seems no hope for him. Offence after offence and sentence after sentence appeared to be the inevitable lot for him or her whose foot had once slipped. Can nothing be done to stop this downward career? I hope that some practical work could (sic) be organised in the police courts, and I enclose five shillings that a fund may be started so that an agent may be appointed to attend the police courts to help the prisoners." (Porter, 1927)

He didn't just send the letter in isolation to Reverend Ellison, he sent with it five shillings which was his donation towards the work. Rainer was not just a talker; he was a doer too!

This was Frederic Rainer's suggestion: CETS should focus on working with the police courts to support those being charged with drink-related offences and crimes. He advised CETS to send representatives to the courts where drink-related offenders were being charged and tried. As I earlier mentioned in this chapter, up until then, a lot of the work of CETS focused on visiting public houses (pubs), cabstands and other public places distributing leaflets, asking people to stop drinking and getting them to sign an abstinence pledge.

Rainer suggested that the church should ask the court to release first-time and sober offenders to these church representatives to befriend, advise, and assist them towards achieving a meaningful, positive and productive life. Through this approach, these church representatives would be able to gain insight into the reasons behind the crime of those who were brought before the courts and what can be done to help them. The members of CETS agreed with Frederic Rainer's suggestion.

Those representatives of the church who were sent to the courts were called London police court missionaries. According to Cassady (2001), "this was the foundation of the working relationship between the church and police courts because it appeared both institutions were fighting a common cause."

Porter (1927) who was a secretary of CETS between 1878 and 1881 carefully outlined the effect of Frederic's letter in his book *Inasmuch*:

"The simple little act of the printer went home. At the very next committee of the C.E.T.S. the suggestion was considered, and in the Report for 1876-1877 comes the sentence, 'Feeling the great need of directing more attention to the real Mission work of the Society, the Southern Province Committee, in August last, appointed a special Missionary, whose duty it should be to visit regularly certain Metropolitan Police Courts for the purpose of dealing with individual drunkards, with a view to their restoration and reclamation.'"

2.2 The work began to grow

By the 1st of August 1876, George Nelson was appointed as the first court missionary of the Southwark and Lambeth courts. In rapid succession, William Batchelor was appointed as the second court missionary the following year. Batchelor was appointed as court missionary of the Bow Street and Mansion House courts. Apparently, both men were ex-Coldstream guards.

Not only were the court missionaries rescuing, supporting, and helping offenders to achieve a more productive lifestyle, but major towns and cities in the United Kingdom also began to embrace the work of police court missionaries. Demand for their services and support began to grow across the country. Such cities included London, Rochester, Lichfield, Liverpool, Manchester, Worcester, and Peterborough. The work of police court missionaries spread like wildfire! It became the order of the day.

Finally, light has come. An intervention that works seems to have been found! Within the first decade of the establishment of the police court missionaries, apart from the extension and the widespread knowledge of their work, two major areas of mission had been achieved. These achievements were indicated in the annual report of the CETS in 1889. The setting up of shelter homes (a little more will be shared about shelter homes in subsequent chapters) and the recruitment of additional paid court missionaries. The minutes of the London CETS Annual Council Meeting held in 1889 reflected these achievements and the zeal of the CETS to build on it: "That the Council beg to suggest to the Executive the desirability of considering a plan by which they be able to promote and stimulate the appointment of police court missionaries and the institution of Shelter Homes in the various diocese."

By 1889, 13 years after the official start-up of their work, CETS had recruited 17 court missionaries. Among them was a female. It became apparent that the presence of a female court missionary was necessary because it was easier for females to work with females. At the annual council meeting, there was a suggestion about mission funds. The mission fund would match the contributions made by the diocese. This funding was necessary for the recruitment of more court missionaries so that the rising need for their work at the police courts would be met. The funds would also be put towards setting up shelters for those who were being supported by court missionaries.

2.3 Making life worth living

As a matter of fact, as of 1884, barely eight years after the work of court missionaries was established, they had supported "1,666 prisoners into accommodation, employment, and emigration. Furthermore, by 1894, number of offenders helped had risen to 15,809." (Jarvis, 1972).

For example, someone like James Mercer, who happened to be one of the police court missionaries from the diocese of Liverpool had made 1,097 daily visits to the police courts and more than 100 prisoners had been supported with free provisions of breakfast (Porter, 1927). It has been suggested that friendly and open relationships (which happen to be part of the secrets of court missionaries) really helped them to support offenders towards reclamation and redemption.

It is important to state that there were efforts from other charitable organisations and groups to help alcohol-related offenders. Several of them recorded success too. However, the outcome of CETS and its court missionaries were in many ways unique and outstanding.

Gradually, the number of alcohol-related charges in courts were reducing and sanity was slowly returning to the streets. Court missionaries were stepping out of the four walls of the church and bringing the desired and needed societal change by looking beyond the short-comings and wrong-doings of offenders. The reasons behind alcoholism were being addressed and people were being rescued from the claws of prison and jail-time.

2.4 Embraced by law

The effectiveness of the police court missionaries had been tested and trusted. It was logical to adopt their work as a national framework. Auerbach (2015) puts it this way: "It stands as an apt demonstration of their indispensability that a succession of Parliamentary Acts was eventually passed recognising both the importance of the duties performed by the missionaries and the value of the agents themselves."

Eventually in 1907, precisely the 8th of May 1907, under the reforming liberal government, Home Office Minister Herbert Samuel pushed for one act in particular and he was successful. The Probation of Offenders Act was passed. It became active from the 1st of January 1908. This act gave court missionaries the official status of 'officers of the court' and they later became known as probation officers. The Home Office had witnessed the effectiveness of the collaboration between the magistrates and the missionaries, and it only made sense for the Home Office minister to take this step.

Through the act, courts were allowed to suspend the punishment of offenders if they enter a period of recognisance, mostly between one to three years. During this one-to-three-year period, the act bestowed power on the court to appoint a named probation officer in the probation order. Part of the duty of the appointed probation officer under the Probation of Offenders Act was to advise, assist and befriend the offender and, when necessary, endeavour to find them a suitable job.

Court missionaries were already doing this for over three decades. Barely two decades after the introduction of the court missionaries, the CETS had paid rent and lodgings for around 495 people, supplied working tools for 581 people, and in around 1,776 instances, they had provided living essentials such as clothing, blankets, coal, and food. These beneficiaries were people who ordinarily would have been sentenced to prison two decades earlier.

The court had no better candidate to fit into the obligations requested by this act than the court missionaries who had already been doing the work successfully for 31 years. As far back as 1889 (18 years before the proposed 1907 Probation of Offenders Act), magistrates themselves had witnessed and trusted the ability of the missionaries to successfully support those charged to court.

"The Magistrates find that they are able to trust the Police Court Missionaries from the beginning, and, instead of sending these poor creatures to prison, they defer judgment, and let the Police Court Missionary try his best, and it happens again and again that, before judgment is passed, the unhappy prisoner has completely changed, and the magistrate inflicts no punishment." (CETS Annual Report 1889, 3).

Furthermore, the Criminal Justice Act of 1925 finally paved the way for police court missionaries to qualify as probation officers. That was how the 49 years of relationship between the missionaries and magistrates was finally cemented, legally. Court missionaries became suitable for the role of probation officers. Porter (1927) puts it this way: "The Act of I925 definitely recognised the Missionary as a suitable probation officer, though in practice he or she had, in a majority of cases, already been appointed to the post."

The Right Reverend and Right Honourable Lord Bishop of London (1901–1939), Arthur Foley Winnington-Ingram, in his foreword for J.Hasloch Porter's book *Inasmuch* stated: "This effort of the Church has taught the State the necessity for a Probation Officer in every police court."

The church took the lead and the nation followed. This was how the church pioneered a social change that had not been experienced before. This all descended from one man, Frederic Rainer, to a group within the church who had the ability to seek change, and then onto the police court. Then eventually their hard work became a blueprint for the nation to follow.

2.5 A typical day in court for the missionaries

The Missionaries Annual Report of 1901 gives a glimpse into what a regular day would look like for court missionaries. In the morning, the court missionary would arrive to court even before the magistrate does, with the intention of having conversations with offenders in the waiting room. They would get a good idea of what the offence is about and why the offender committed the offence. They can sympathise with the offenders and oftentimes this time spent with the offender would help court missionaries to find offenders who are sober and remorseful. By the time the magistrate arrives at the court and starts hearing cases for the day, the court missionary already has an idea of each case.

During hearings, the magistrate would turn to the court missionary to hear their opinion about the case or to ask court missionaries for help with making additional enquiries which would guide the magistrate towards making the correct judgment. Sometimes, magistrates would confer with court missionaries during lunch time for their view on certain cases (CETS Annual Report 1902).

According to Auerbach (2015), "many a time the Missionary, by his efforts, is able to avert evil or prevent the summons from being taken out by effecting a reconciliation." Auerbach further states that magistrates would often turn to court missionaries again and again, sometimes even handing over cases to the court missionaries.

In the same year of 1901, magistrates handed over 2,000 cases to court missionaries to handle. These were cases of offenders who would have ordinarily been imprisoned for their offence. These are lives that would have gone to prison and come out as the same or worse than they were before going to prison. These people ended up experiencing a much more positive life with better outcomes. Therefore, court missionaries became part and parcel of daily proceedings in court.

A few years after the establishment of court missionaries, it was glaringly obvious to the magistrates that their government's approach towards using imprisonment to rehabilitate minor offenders was no longer advisable, and it wasn't feasible either. A better approach had already been discovered. The results and outcomes were obvious for everyone to see. As a matter of fact, by the time the results of the court missionaries were being seen in society, the magistrates had no choice but to start putting funds into the missionaries' work out of the police court's limited resources. It was estimated that the courts gave a yearly amount of £5 to £15 to the court missionaries. As if that was not enough, another £1 to £5 was donated by each magistrate from their own personal funds (CETS Annual Reports 1890 and 1891).

By 1902, both men and women court missionaries had conducted well over 37,000 interviews in the courts and had attended police court proceedings on 1,334 occasions. The missionaries were serving both magistrates and offenders. They were working for the magistrates by conducting preliminary interviews and would advise magistrates on a case-by-case basis based on the information they received from the friendly and compassionate interviews. While, on the other hand, they were able to present the cases of individual offenders before the magistrate and advocate for mercy on behalf of the offenders, after which they would offer counsel and aid to the offenders.

Of course, from the late 1880s, court missionaries were beginning to receive innumerable amounts of testimonials. For some top officials within the United Kingdom's criminal justice structure, the level of achievement was unbelievable. Some of these officials wrote to the court missionaries to express their undeniable gratitude. One such letter is shared below. The magistrate John Dickinson wrote of his gratitude and that of his colleague Frederic Meade: "The work in such a Court as Thames, and in such a poor and densely populated district as this, must necessarily be very heavy, but your energy, attention, and kindly sympathy have never failed. Your work is a great one, helping the weak and tempted, comforting the miserable and hopeless, and striving to rescue the forlorn and vicious." (CETS Annual Report 1890).

The pressure on the magistrates was beginning to reduce. Offenders who ought to have been behind bars were now having kind-hearted Christians holding them by the hand and restoring their hope. Rent was being paid; people were getting the tools they needed to start a trade. Normally, people were jailed for vagrancy, but the church was providing alternatives to that! They were providing shelters to solve the problem of vagrancy. Boys' shelters were provided for young people, as well as vulnerable women.

One of the most heartwarming CETS annual report I read is the 1915 report. This was during the first World War.

"Perhaps the best report we have to give for the last year," the author wrote, "will be found in the large number of men and lads who have passed through the hands of the Missionaries in the last year or two, and having been under their probation or care, instead of being sent to prison, have now joined the Colours and are doing their best for King and Country. Over 1,100 who have been under our Missionaries 'quite recently,' have joined the Army and Navy since the war began." (CETS Annual Report 1915, 21).

Over 1,100 people who would have been sent to prison and possibly become a burden to society ended up being defenders of the nation. They stood for the nation during one of the most difficult and vulnerable times, a time of war. All because they were lucky to receive the help and support of court missionaries. It is indeed heartwarming.

2.6 The end of LPCM

Around 1938, probation support was transferred to official agents of the state and the Home Office took up the responsibility of recruiting and training probation officers. There were concerns from certain quarters of government that probation was too sensitive and important to be left in the hands of "religiously motivated amateurs" (Porter, 1927). As a result, the Home Office took over the affairs of probation and there have been several evolutions in the probation service since then.

Chapter 3
19th century faith pioneers of change

When talking about Frederic Rainer, Cassady (2001) clearly states: "Little is written about the man who is said to have taken that first step, and few beyond the areas of probation know of his work."

As I stated in the abstract, it was a struggle for me to get adequate material on both Frederic Rainer and the input of the Church in the development of the probation system in the UK. As a matter of fact, I came across materials that made attempts to trivialise the effect of the great works of Frederic Rainer. There is a big lesson for the Church right here — document your work! The Christian community must work with posterity in mind. I know it's been debated in certain quarters whether the Bible demands that charitable works must, or must not, be done for public recognition. However, the motive here isn't for public recognition, it is for subsequent generations to have a template and a guide to follow when continuing what the earlier generations began. I hope this book will serve as such a guide for present and emerging generations.

3.1 The man, Frederic Rainer

Frederic Rainer was the last of six children in his family. His father's name was George and his mother's name was Susannah. His dad was a Mason and Susannah was a local coffee shop proprietor. Frederic Rainer was born in 1836 in Windsor, United Kingdom. He attended a national school. National schools were established in the 19th century, in the year 1811.

The National Society for Promoting Religious Education was instrumental to the creation of national schools. This was a Church of England body in England and Wales for the promotion of church schools and Christian education. Their aim was that "the National Religion should be made the foundation of National Education and should be the first and chief thing taught to the poor, according to the excellent Liturgy and Catechism provided by our Church."

When I came across this in my research, I began to reflect; could it be that Frederic Rainer's education played a part in the way he thought? Could it be that he had been taught the message of compassion and love as a part of Christian ethics? Could the education he received from the national school have informed his behavior and reaction to social issues? Does the Church and Christian Organisations begin to think of Christian schools again? An academic institution where the thinking of children are shaped towards divine compassion?

Frederic Rainer left school in 1851 after which he got a job at the Windsor Express Office. It wasn't long after that in January 1852 that Rainer decided to pursue apprenticeship as a printer. In 1862, Frederic got married to Louisa and they both had strong love for each other. Shortly after their wedding, Frederic and Louisa moved to the city of London. It was in London that Frederic picked up a job working for Messrs. Gilbert and Rivington, ecclesiastical printers. Frederic was proud of this new achievement, and he committed his strength and energy to his new job and executed his duties diligently. The organisation was based in Holborn.

It was recorded that Frederic Rainer hardly used public transport when he lived and worked in London. Most of the time, he walked. Therefore, it's easy to assume that it was during this period of walking across different places and communities in London that he started to notice the extent of the decay on the streets. He began to witness the lives of people who lived hopelessly without purpose or any sense of direction due to alcohol addiction. This was a snapshot of what was happening in other communities throughout the United Kingdom. Frederic's heart began to bleed. Just like we see on our high streets and town centres these days; Rainer saw people whose lives were being destroyed by drunkenness and alcohol addiction and he was moved to compassion.

It is also on record that Frederic Rainer was artistic and creative. This is because a few poems were found in his archive. Through his poems, it is easy to understand his thoughts and purpose. Frederic Rainer wrote a poem titled *Give Him a pull Brother, out of the stream*:

"Strong drink's the current that hurrying down.
Thousands of votaries year after year;
Shall we stand helpless and leave them to drown?
Is there no possible remedy near?
Bring them the life-belt of Abstinence, friend; Carefully, prayerfully, be this our theme –
Give them a hand, brother, gently yet firm; Give them a pull, brother, out of the
stream." (Porter, 1927)

It is quite easy to feel the pulse of Frederic Rainer in this poem. There isn't much difference between the tone of this poem and the lines from his letter (which I shared in previous chapters) to Reverend Ellison. It was his life pursuit, and he went all the way to see it happen. Undoubtedly, this theme must have been ringing in his mind for a long time. I don't doubt the possibility of him having sleepless nights on this matter. The same applies to the secret prayer of Sir Robert Peel which I will share later in this chapter.

3.2 Strength of the 1st rescue mission

Rainer clearly was a man of passion and prayer because it reflected in his poem: "Bring them the life-belt of Abstinence, friend; Carefully, prayerfully, be this our theme." It is obvious that the root of Frederic Rainer's ideology wasn't just from his head, it was straight from the heart. Prayer played a huge part in the success story of the English probation system. It's a truth we can't shy away from.

His poem showed what was going on in his mind. He knew "lending a hand carefully and prayerfully. Giving the vulnerable a helping hand, gently yet firm" was how to drive change. "Lending a hand" is the physical step taken to get the work done. Being "prayerful" was the secret power that guided and guarded the physical steps being taken. Prayer laid a foundation for the work, and prayer sustained the work. This is a great lesson to learn if we want to pioneer change in our society.

God is the bedrock of the ideology of the probation system. Is it any wonder it earned excellent results when it was carried out accordingly by the early court missionaries?

"Whatever is good and perfect is a gift coming down to us from God our Father, who created all the lights in the heavens. He never changes or casts a shifting shadow." James 1:17 **(New Living Translation)**

The English probation system was God's good and perfect gift to the nation to help rescue all the lives that were being destroyed by alcohol and the severe punishment brought upon those "whose feet slipped."

Society is at that point again when we need another rescue mission, carried out by those who have a drive to see lives changed and our society and communities transformed.

Like the Rainer's' and Peel's' of the 19th century, it must start with fervent prayers and physical action to begin the transformation we desire.

3.3 His mentorship connection

Fortunately for Rainer, he formed a cordial relationship with Reverend Ellison. Reverend Ellison, at the time, was the Vicar of Windsor. Reverend Ellison developed an interest in Rainer and Rainer became his protégé. Due to his kind heart and compassion, it's easy to assume that Frederic Rainer had a likeable personality. So, it wasn't strange when he became very dear to Reverend Ellison.
Around this time, Reverend Ellison himself was beginning to pay a lot of attention to temperance and gave ministerial efforts towards the same.

It is said that Reverend Ellison encouraged Rainer to be actively involved in the work of the CETS. This was good news for Rainer who, first-hand, had already seen the struggle of addiction on the streets of London and developed an undeniable passion for them. He took up the offer joyfully and became involved with the temperance endeavour of CETS. In 1876, Frederic Rainer put pen to paper and wrote to Reverend Ellison:

"Once a person got into trouble through drink or other cause, there seems no hope for him. Offence after offence and sentence after sentence appeared to be the inevitable lot for him or her whose foot had once slipped. Can nothing be done to stop this downward career? I hope that some practical work could (sic) be organised in the police courts, and I enclose five shillings that a fund may be started so that an agent may be appointed to attend the police courts to help the prisoners." (Porter, 1927)

Not only did Frederic Rainer put his purpose on paper, he also included a donation of five shillings to facilitate the work. He suggested that the CETS should step up their work by working directly with the courts where alcohol-related offenders were being tried. Prior to this time, the CETS were largely focusing on distributing tracts in cabstands, pubs and public houses and encouraging people to quit drinking and sign pledges of abstinence. However, they didn't record a lot of success.

Therefore, through the idea and donations of Frederic Rainer, the CETS turned their attention towards working with the police courts directly. Then, the change gradually began! The CETS had the responsibility of recruiting and managing the affairs of court missionaries. The first court missionary employed in 1876 was George Nelson.

3.4 The case for youth involvement

The involvement of Frederic Rainer in the work of the Church of England Temperance Society (CETS) brought innovation and positive outcomes. Rainer was around 40 years of age when he made his recommendation about Court/Church collaboration and his donations.

It is obvious that Churches and Christian faith groups need to start involving young people in their strategic and management drive. Young people bring innovation and other ways of achieving goals. Innovation does not necessarily disrupt planning; it just brings an alternative means of getting work done. Since we live in a digital age, there is plenty of room for young people to maximise their potential.

Tract sharing still stands as a major means for Churches to share the missionary message of Hope. This must continue. However, an innovation stirred by the emerging generation must be given a chance. There are young people who are idle with incredible talents and abilities that are relevant for reaching the unreached.

Frederic Rainer's involvement and innovation brought a solution and became a national footprint. There are lots of untapped potential in the emerging generation waiting for exploration.

3.5 Fifty years of uncommon impact

At the celebration of the CETS jubilee in 1926, a lot of commendations were showered on Frederic Rainer and his endeavors through the CETS. Important personalities starting from His Majesty the King commended the "admirable work done by the Police Court Mission." He went on to say that the works of the Police Court Mission "has won the highest encomiums from judges, magistrates, police officials and Christian social workers of all denominations."

Another remarkable commendation rendered at the jubilee celebration of the Police Court Mission reads below: "In this land of ours thirty years ago there were 66 prisons, today there are 32. Thirty years ago, before the Probation of Offenders Act came into force, there were 33,000 prisoners ... today there are 11,000 ... [and it was] hoped that in thirty years' time ... [there would be] no prisoners at all."

The work carried out by police court missionaries eventually reduced the number of prisons in the United Kingdom by half, while the number of prisoners were reduced by more than 70 per cent. That is reformation and transformation!

3.6 Rainer was unstoppable

As discussed earlier in this chapter, Rainer was married to Louisa and the couple were happy together. Their marriage was blessed with eight children. However, only six of those children survived past childhood. If Frederic had such heart and passion for the vulnerable, how much more would he feel for his own children? He lost two children while they were still growing. However, his passion and commitment to the redemption and reclamation of the vulnerable and downtrodden was not compromised.

Rainer established two CETS branches in Hertfordshire, and both branches conducted amazing remedial work to restore offenders to a life of productivity. The work of the court missionaries was a life commitment for Rainer. Frederic pursued the goal of the Police Court Mission despite his own share of life circumstances. This is commendable and should serve as motivation to every one of us. We can still lead a productive life regardless of what life throws at us.

3.7 Sir Robert Peel, his legacy of peace in England and Ireland

Sir Robert Peel served as the Chief Secretary of Ireland between August 1812 to August 1818. He was the Home Secretary from 1822 until 1827 and then came back into office as Home Secretary again between 1828 and 1830. He later served as a two-time Prime Minister of England between 1834 and 1835 and then again from 1841 to 1846 (Larkin, 2022).

His passion for peace and order was evident in his track record of establishing the Peace Preservation Force in Ireland when he was the Chief Secretary. During the late 18th century to the early 19th century, Ireland suffered a lot of insurgencies. However, in 1814 Sir Robert Peel was successful in his bid to see the Peace Preservation Force introduced in Ireland. This act permitted the appointment of superintending magistrates and additional constables in troubled areas of Ireland. This was a great development that brought about the restoration of peace in Ireland.

Until 1829, all that existed in England in terms of a police force were unpaid constables who had limited ability in crime intelligence and investigation. In situations of serious public disorder, the army intervened. Available historical sources stated that some of the unpaid constables from before 1829 had issues with alcohol addiction themselves.

Eventually, just as he successfully did in Ireland, Sir Robert Peel was successful in getting the Metropolitan Police Act signed into law in June 1829. This act saw the formal introduction of the London Metropolitan Police. These were paid and trained personnel who were held directly accountable to the Home Secretary.

This was another welcome development. Even though it didn't solve the entire problem of crime and alcohol addiction completely, it was a start in the right direction. By the time Sir Robert Peel left office as Home Secretary in 1830, he had positively impacted the outlook of policing in England just as he did in Ireland.

3.8 Amazing discovery

Sir Robert Peel studied Classics and Mathematics at Christ Church, Oxford (a constituent college of the University of Oxford). He was born to a rich family whose predominant business was textile manufacturing. Sir Robert Peel was another Christian who built significant social structures that re-defined the security and preservation of law and order in England and Ireland. Due to the significant role he played in establishing the Metropolitan Police, police were called *peelers* in England (linked to his surname), and *bobbies* in Ireland (a term I have often heard in England too).

Sir Robert Peel was part of the Church of England. He died in June 1850, three days after falling during a horse ride and sustaining significant injury. After his death, there was an amazing discovery in his private drawer; his secret written prayer to God:

"Great and Merciful God, ruler of all nations, help me daily to repair to Thee for wisdom and grace suitable to the high office whereto Thy providence has called me. Strengthen, 0 Lord, my natural powers and faculties, that the weighty and solemn interests with which Thy servant is charged may not greatly suffer through weakness of body and confusion of mind. Deign, I beseech Thee, to obviate or correct the ill-effects of such omissions or mistakes in my proceedings as may result from partial knowledge, infirmity of judgment, or unfaithfulness in any with whom I may have to do.

Let Thy blessing rest upon my Sovereign and my country. Dispose the hearts of all in high stations to adopt such measures as will preserve public order, foster industry, and alleviate distress. May true religion flourish, and peace be universal. Grant that, so far as may consist with human weakness, whatever is proposed by myself or others for the general good may be viewed with candour, and that all new and useful measures may be conducted to a prosperous issue.

As for me, Thy servant, grant, 0 Merciful God, that I may not be so engrossed with public anxieties as that Thy word should become unfruitful in me, or be so moved by difficulty or opposition as not to pursue the narrow way which leadeth me to life. And, 0 most gracious Father, if, notwithstanding my present desires and purposes, I should forget Thee, do not Thou forget me, seeing that I entreat Thy constant remembrance and favour only for the sake of our most blessed Advocate and Redeemer Jesus Christ, to whom with Thee and the Holy Spirit be glory for ever. Amen." (Webber, 2004).

You can feel his love for the nation in his prayer. You can see his reliance on God for a prosperous and safe England. His prayers show that it takes more than knowledge to build positive, life-changing institutions and social structures. It is obvious that Sir Robert Peel didn't rely just on his knowledge when executing his official duties throughout all the public service positions he held in his lifetime. In the first paragraph of his prayer, he displayed his reliance on God for wisdom to discharge his duties. He called his duties "solemn and weighty," he understood that the task of governance is a sensitive and enormous one. Therefore, he asked for God's help against wrong judgment and human frailty.

The second paragraph of his prayer was solely for the nation. He prayed for everyone in the position of authority "to adopt such measures as will preserve public order, foster industry, and alleviate distress." His desire for peace and order shone through his prayers. He prayed to God for the blessing and prosperity of England.

The third and final verse of his prayer is very powerful. He finally closed his prayer by saying that he won't let the difficulty and challenge of his "official position" take him away from the Lord. He said he is in the habit of always asking God for His favour and kindness because he knew how frail he is as a human being.

Sir Robert Peel served in three different sensitive positions both in England and Ireland: Chief Secretary in Ireland, Home Secretary in England twice and Prime Minister in England twice! It was obvious he depended on God through prayers. The answer to his prayers reflected in the outcome of his work. This is the secret of his success. Obviously, his tenure in all three offices may not have been flawless but his significant achievements are undeniable. These are huge lessons given to us by two faith pioneers of change. They are, and they have given, a visible and feasible template for the next rescue mission to follow.

Chapter 4
Rebuilding the broken walls of society

In May 2022, the outcome, and recommendations from an independent review on children's social care was published. The independent review was commissioned by the United Kingdom's government and was led by Josh MacAlister. The comprehensive report is available on the government website. According to the UK parliament website, part of the major findings of this independent review was that without concrete change and adjustment to the current system, the number of children in care would increase from 80,000 to 100,000 within ten years.

The parliament website reports further: "The review's final report argued that the current children's social care system was 'increasingly skewed to crisis intervention, with outcomes for children that continue to be unacceptably poor and costs that continue to rise.'" It concluded that "for these reasons, a radical reset is now unavoidable."

Not only does the report indicate that children's social care in the country is unacceptably poor, but it also indicates that the cost of maintaining it is rising. The report strongly recommends a "radical reset."

4.1 The government makes the same suggestion as court missionaries.

The government reacted to Josh MacAlister's independent review with a plan to improve children's social care. The plan which was themed *Stable Homes: built on love* contained the government decision to focus on family help, keeping children safer, supporting families to help children, making care better for children and helping care leavers. The government reiterated that "Every child deserves to grow in a safe, stable and loving home."

The government reached the same conclusion as the early court missionaries; that children need a stable home that is built on love to thrive. It is true, every child deserves to grow up in a safe, stable, and loving home. Later in this chapter I will discuss how the Church of England Temperance Society built inebriate homes and why they intentionally called them *homes*.

The inebriate homes were built as places where children could access the love they needed to thrive. I have compiled some real-life experiences of young and vulnerable boys and girls who used these homes and the impact it had on their lives.

It is increasingly evident that it is difficult to discuss real social change without putting an emphasis on divine compassion.

The government need not to look any further, the right direction at this crucial time is the Church and other Christian organisations. The government's decision to facilitate stable homes built on love is absolutely the right choice, however, there is no better place to find the right partner for this task than the Church and Christian organisations. Like the 19th century police court missionaries, they possess the exact same natural inclination and motivation of divine compassion and unrivalled love.

4.2 Remodeling homes, reconciling couples

In 1895, the Court of Summary Jurisdiction and the Metropolitan Police Court were given the power to deal with matrimonial matters (Porter, 1927). In simple terms, the magistrate was vested with the power to grant judicial separation. Before long, this became another workload on courts. Courts started becoming packed with tons and tons of couples hoping to be granted judicial separation. The workload around judicial separation was becoming huge.

By this time, court missionaries had gained the confidence of magistrates, and were able to give a helping hand in this regard. Therefore, it wasn't a surprise when magistrates started seeking the assistance of court missionaries in marital matters that would come before the court.

"One of the most common tasks of missionaries was mediating between aggrieved spouses when one felt compelled to seek a court summons against the other, most typically for assault, abuse, or neglect." (Porter, 1927)

Therefore, apart from reclaiming those brought before the magistrates for alcohol-related offences, court missionaries were deployed by magistrates to help in preserving family values through mediation.

"The essence of the work is the personal contact of a kindly, experienced, Christian man or woman with those in need of help. Results are striking, even splendid, especially among women and children. Changed lives, remodeled homes, married couples reconciled, and the shipwreck of young lives averted are daily occurrences." (Porter, 1927)

This is part of the foundation on which the early court missionaries built their relationship with the magistrates in the 19th century. They needed to provide what the government and society needed: S*table homes: built on love.*

The family unit was falling apart. The magistrates thought no one else was more fit for the job of rescuing such families than the court missionaries. According to Porter's statement above, court missionaries, through their intervention at police courts, remodeled homes and reconciled married couples. The desired result of both was "averting the shipwreck of young lives."

When families break, lives are broken too. The men and women in these families, and especially the children, suffer significantly. Broken family relationships lead to a broken society. It leads to the shipwreck of young innocent lives.

This is a huge task for the next rescue mission. Family values, much like the 19th century, is fast falling apart. The collapse of the family institution is the collapse of society. A strong family institution is the foundation for a strong society. Unfortunately, we are fast losing out on family values in our society.

Court missionaries understood the importance of strong family values. They understood that God has vested interest in the unity and sanctity of marriage. That is why court missionaries were interested in family values and stability, and they paid the price to see broken families be restored. They understood that strong families make strong communities. Like other aspects of their work, court missionaries were successful in restoring family values!

Porter (1927), when analysing the court missionaries' report on family and home reconciliation gave this analysis:

"One Missionary reports thirty reconciliations during the year, another forty, several give higher figures, some content themselves with the word 'many,' but I have never yet seen a report which omits all reference to this side of the work. Be it remembered that there are 181 Missionaries working under the Church of England Temperance Society."

That was the level of success that the court missionaries had achieved. They rescued many marriages from the brink of collapse. In the world we now live in, family values appear to be at the brink of collapse. However, the examples set by the court missionaries gives evidence that rescue is possible.

4.3 Testimonies and strategies

I am sharing the true-life experiences of people who have benefitted from the efforts of early court missionaries to save homes and families.

A 9-year hopelessly broken home restored!

A 40-year-old woman had been separated from her husband because she was suffering from alcohol addiction. She had two children who are 18 and 10 years old. Her ex-husband had sole custody of these children. The woman was eventually arrested and charged for stealing, but, fortunately for her, she was handed over to a court missionary for a period of 12 months. She was eligible for probation because it was her first time in court.

The court missionary took this woman, had a long, friendly conversation with her and advised her to think beyond herself and think of the implications that her actions would have on her children. According to records, the missionary urged her to think of "her responsibility to God" for her children. The woman decided to deal with her addiction issues with the support of the missionary.

The court missionary found accommodation for her, got her a job as a carer which she carried out until the end of her 12-month probation. The court missionary even went as far as to speak with her ex-husband and children about the tremendous progress made by the woman and that was how she was reconciled with the family she had lost for nine years!

4.4 Averting the shipwreck of young lives

Children often suffer the most consequences as a result of broken families. Josh MacAlister's findings recommended that an additional £2.6B investment is required over the next four years to fix the issues within children's social care.

Not only is the breakdown of the family having a negative impact on children's social care, it is also affecting the quality of life that people have after the fact. This will also cause an adverse effect on the country's socio-economic life, because the more we see a breakdown of family values, the more the government will have to spend on children's social care. As I stated at the start of this chapter, evidence from Josh MacAlister's independent review suggests that the number of children in care will rise to 100,000 within the next ten years if there is no radical reset.

Unexpected life events such as the breakdown of a relationship has led to homelessness in the United Kingdom (Shelter, 2023). Prison and care-leavers are also forced into homelessness (Crisis, 2023).

Action for Children is a global charity that protects and supports children and young people through the provision of practical and emotional care and support. They have provided some alarming insights.
In 2021, eight out of ten young people that were helped into homeless accommodation in Dorset said that their situation

was due to the breakdown of their family relationship. One in six young homeless people take part in illegal activity in order to have somewhere to stay.

Young homeless people have become victims of exploitation and violence. I will share a little more insight on this in Chapter 5, when I explain the results of another independent review which shows how children in this category are being recruited into drug supply and use.

I have witnessed a couple of instances of broken families in my work in the community where both partners find love elsewhere. Then the children are left in the care of an aged grandparent. However, those grandparents struggle to look after these children because they (who are often in their 70s or 80s) lack enough physical and mental capacity and ability to care for them effectively. In situations such as this, where the breakdown of the family leads to the neglect of the children, they might begin to engage in crime or other life-wrecking habits. Children found in situations such as this need love to thrive. The type of love found within a loving family.

4.5 Personal experience

I once managed a food bank, and a teenage boy who had been brought up by a single mum used to follow his mum whenever she visited. Each time they came by, I took the time to chat with him and he'd tell me about his schoolwork and life aspirations. I must tell you, he was very ambitious. To my surprise, even though he belonged to another faith, he presented me with a hand-made Easter card that particular year. This was how I found out he was talented in making cards. I was so pleased.

When he went back to school in September that year, he was sad because the council had moved him and his mum to another council flat farther from his school. The best options for him were either to move schools or get a bicycle. He had already moved schools numerous times because they had been moved from one house to another. So I suggested, "Why don't you make some birthday cards and I'll sell them to friends and colleagues so you can raise some money?" He took up the idea and made some beautiful cards. I sold them, and he was able to raise money for a bicycle. The expression of joy, screaming and jumping when I handed him the money will stay with me a long time.

This is what builds joy and brings hope to vulnerable children and families. This is what is needed to fulfil the government's ambition for having stable homes built on love.

Court missionaries left no stone unturned when remodeling homes. Court missionaries provided accommodation for children who were neglected or were victims of broken family relationships. It is on record that court missionaries didn't just provide housing for those who lacked shelter, but they made a home out of their accommodation provision. You may want to ask me how?

Court missionaries called their accommodation provisions *home* because they felt that the absence of family and home-life contributed to the shipwreck of the lives of young people. So, to the court missionaries, these young people must be provided with an environment where they can be shown love and care like every other child.

There were several residential projects (homes) for boys and girls. These were either directly established by court missionaries or established and managed in collaboration with them. Some of them were known as:

The Home for Inebriate Men at Caldecote (inebriate means to be drunk or intoxicated), the Home for Lads, Padcroft

Yiewsley, Boys' Garden Colony Basingstoke, Boys' Shelter Home Camberwell, St. George's Home for Lads Chester, Grove House (Boys' Home) Manchester, Manchester Training Farm (Lads) Barrow, Frederick House (Boys' Home) Chatham, Home for Boys Bath City, Boys' Club Plymouth, and Lindum Lodge (for Boys) Lincoln.

4.6 Boys' Shelter Home, Camberwell

Court missionaries were intentional when rescuing children and young people. They made every effort to save young offenders from the path of prison sentence. I must make it clear that it was not because they wanted to encourage crime among children and young people, but because they knew these children and young people would come out from prison even worse than when they went in. Porter (1927) confirmed this in his writing:

"Mere children were sent to prison as a matter of course, notwithstanding the fact that the prisons were dens of iniquity and schools of crime. The lessons were usually well learnt, and 'once a criminal always a criminal' was the almost invariable rule."

I will share a few inspiring examples of how court missionaries turned around the lives of young boys who were helplessly heading in the wrong direction in life with little to no hope.
I have two aims for doing this. Firstly, to give an idea of the amount of work that was done (and still needs to be done), and secondly, to let you know that redemption is possible.

4.7 From failed home to a fulfilled life

Police court missionaries had suggested a home for boys in South London. The reason for this suggestion was that the home would be a place to house and assist young boys who had been charged at court until another institution, or work, could be arranged.

Fortunately, a lady donated the sum of £350 to the project on the condition of anonymity. The CETS struggled to get a suitable property for the project, because a lot of landlords turned them down once they heard that the property was going to be used to house young boys who were being charged at court.

Eventually, the CETS found a dilapidated building (34 Camberwell Road). For many years, the building had served as a day and boarding school facility. They purchased the freehold and a few years after that, they refurbished the entire building. In 1913, the new building was opened. Within the first 30 years of establishing the home, they had housed and provided 2,560 young boys with a fresh start.

A touching example was given about a young man that was caught wandering the streets. Apparently, his parents had separated. Both his mother and father had new partners with whom they lived, and neither of them wanted the boy. He was handed over to the court missionaries and he was housed at the Boys' Shelter Home in Camberwell. The Police Court Mission secured him a job on a farm in Yorkshire, but they had to bring him back after two days because he couldn't cope due to his health condition. Unfortunately, the boy suffered from a terrible case of asthma, which made it difficult for him to hold down any sort of work for a long period of time.

The boy lived in the Boys Home in Camberwell for over a year, until one day, an ex-boy returned from his job on the sea and suggested taking this lad with him. The boy was happy, and he loved it! He secured a job in the ships' kitchen and started a new blossoming life. He would come back to the Boys Home after every trip until he finally decided to settle down in New Zealand and got himself a job in a hotel. During the first world war, he paid a visit to the Camberwell Boys Home as a member of the forces in New Zealand. He had joined the forces and was fighting in France at the time.

4.8 They are no longer fatherless robbers

Two boys were once charged for stealing. They stole money and were handed over to court missionaries who took them to one of the Boys' Homes. They were looked after and given a sense of family love. Within a short period of time, both boys had settled down. The elder brother got a job on a steamer (steamers were ships that were powered by steam engines), and he later achieved his dream of becoming a sailor! The youngest got a job in Yorkshire working in a coal mine. These boys would have been jailed and could possibly have become real robbers after their jail-time.

In addition, the court missionaries re-united them with their father.

4.9 Court missionaries' work with women and girls

Between 1884 and 1885 it became necessary for the Police Court Missionaries to start recruiting women. This is because women work well with children, girls, and other women. The first female court missionary was appointed in Liverpool. This was the beginning of a whole new development to the work of the missionaries.

Before long, the court missionaries had around eight female employees and two female volunteers. Within one year, they had conducted around 14,000 visits surrounding court cases and attended 1,334 court sittings. Their service to female offenders was very commendable.

4.10 Found real life after suicide attempt

The parents of a young girl decided to separate when she was four years old. After this, she passed from one family member to another. By the time she became a teenager, she was frustrated and decided to end her life. She had never once experienced the love and care that every child deserves. So, she decided to jump into a river in an attempt at suicide. Fortunately, there were policemen around who rescued her.

After she was rescued, the policemen handed her over to a female police court missionary and she was put into a Girls' Home. The Girls' Home decided it would be best to send her to a training school. At this point, all suicidal tendencies had apparently disappeared. For the first time ever, she felt loved and cared for like every other child. The chaplain of her temporary home made her realise that God had a reason for saving her life, and that's why the policemen rescued her. The warmth, the love, and the care made so much difference to the girl and changed her life immeasurably. Eventually, the girl would write:
"One thing I realise now is that I have got plenty of kind friends, and there is never any need to do as I did before. I want to try to help others. My ambition is to be a Missionary."

4.11 All she needed was a chance.

A female police court missionary once found an 18-year-old girl who had been in prison before and was in court again. Due to her previous imprisonment, it was most likely that she would be sentenced again. Her parents had died, meaning she was an orphan who had to fend for herself. The police court missionary pleaded for the girl to be released on bail for 12 months. Her plea was granted.

Again, she was taken to a Girls' Home where she was warmly received. Nobody cared that she was an ex-inmate. All everybody saw was a vulnerable teenager who needed love and a family, and so she was shown love the way she had never received it.

It wasn't long before she got a job as a parlour-maid, which we would know now as a waiter. The commendation of her manager at work was incredible. The girl later had this to write about her experience with the police court missionary: "You have given me the only chance I ever had in my life, and I am going to take it."

It is much easier to build families than to fix the implications of a broken one. It costs more to fix the consequences of a family breakdown than to ensure the stability and sanctity of family values.

Judging by the sad stories shared by both children in care and children who have left care in Josh MacAlister's report, the government needs people who have intrinsic love and are motivated by divine compassion like the early court missionaries to help get this work done.

Of course, some type of training will be required so that the administrative and ethical obligations of social care is understood by Churches and Christian organisations who provide, or are willing to provide, this support. However, we can't shy away from the fact that we need the same kind of love that was displayed by the Christian community, through the early court missionaries, showered on vulnerable young boys and girls.

PART 2

Chapter 5
The scourge is here again

"It's clear that the old way of doing things isn't working." (Rt.Hon. Boris Johnson, 2021)

Boris Johnson, the former UK Prime Minister, made the above declaration about the state of the nation in relation to drug addiction and its socio-economic impact on the country. This was captured in a vital document called *From harm to hope: a 10 year drugs plan to cut crime and save lives* published in December 2021.

The government commissioned Professor Dame Carol Black to carry out an independent review of the current impact that drug addiction is having on the country. Part of her task was to recommend a way forward in terms of the treatment and recovery of those who are struggling with drug addiction. The government wanted a new evidence-based approach in tackling drug use and the harm associated with it.

In her findings, Prof. Dame Carol Black declared that the current government provisions for tackling drug addiction are "inadequate" and not "fit for purpose."

Through her findings, it is evident that the scourge is here again. I will share a relevant summary of the outcome of Professor Dame Carol Black's independent review and her recommendations.

5.1 The 21st century social plague

Professor Dame Carol Black's independent review came in two parts. The first part was published on the 27th of February 2020. The first part of her findings explains the extent of the damage that drug use, supply and demand has caused individuals and families within the UK, and even on the UK's economy.

I have personally analysed her findings into three categories for readers to easily understand:

5.2 Drug use

As of 2019, there were around three million drug users in England and Wales. Around 300,000 people in England had used extremely harmful drugs including opiates and/or cocaine. The UK's illicit drug market is worth almost £10b and has an increasingly exploitative supply chain. Drug-related deaths have increased by 80 per cent since 2012. In 2018, one out of every three 15-year-olds had reportedly used drugs. Half of all homicides and acquisitive crimes are linked to drugs.

People with a serious drug addiction occupy one in three prison places. This statistic in particular links back to previous chapters, as in the 19th century three quarters of prison cells were loaded with female alcohol-related offenders.

High drug use is linked to deprivation and poverty. High drug use is also linked to premature death, and this occurs disproportionately more in deprived areas and the north of the country. There has been a tremendous increase in the use of new psychoactive substances amongst homeless people, those in prison, and people under the age of 30. Around 220,000 adults use drugs daily.

A huge number of young people and children have recently been pulled into drug supply and use. Some 27,000 young people now identify as gang members with serious links to drug dealing.

Organised crime groups and an advancement in technology has greatly influenced the supply of drugs coming into the UK. 1,716 organised crime groups supply illicit drugs in the country including in UK prisons.

Most drugs used in the UK are produced outside of the country.

The county line model has overtaken the heroin and cocaine retail market. County lines have been driving the increase of violence in the drug market as well as the exploitation of young people and vulnerable drug users. County lines are defined as a "form of criminal activity in which drug dealers in major cities establish networks for the supply and sale of drugs to users in towns and rural areas, using other people (typically those who are young or otherwise vulnerable) to carry, store, and sell the drugs." (Oxford Dictionary)

A dramatic increase in homelessness and the rising demand on children's social care has often been linked to drug addiction. Targeted support work needs to be done with young people (especially those under the age of 30), those battling homelessness, those currently in prison, people who have recently been released from prison, and those who are living in deprived areas or experiencing deprivation.

5.3 Suggested cause of drug use

Poverty and deprivation have been found to be some of the core drivers behind the demand for opiates and cocaine. Child poverty appears to be one of the major causes behind the recruitment of children into county lines. Dame Carol

Black suggested that the demand for drugs is linked to the night-time economy, this would include industries that are linked with nightlife such as bars, nightclubs, and pubs. Drugs are widely available and accessible in UK prisons. Around 15 per cent of prisoners test positive in random drug tests. Prisons often have a limited amount of activity for prisoners. Male local and category C prisons (often categorised as low-risk prisons) seem to experience this challenge more.

The high number of children in care, school exclusions and the rampant increase of social media influence has been said to have played a major role in this surge.

5.4 Gaps within government provisions that are contributing to the surge in drug use

Restricting the drug supply has been incredibly difficult because the institutions who would be responsible for it are experiencing budget cuts.

More than a third of people in prison are jailed for addiction-related offences, such as burglary, shoplifting etc. These prisoners are more likely to serve a short period of time in jail, therefore their prison treatment and the way they are released back into the community is oftentimes extremely poor. This poor attempt at rehabilitation often means they are very likely to re-offend.

The reduction in the budget of local governments means they now have a limited ability to provide adequate treatment. Some local authorities have reduced their expenditure by 40 per cent. This means there is also a shortage of staff and experts. "Local Authorities normally work with NHS Trust and not-for-profit Organisations to provide treatment. However, because the funding of both NHS Trusts and not-for-profit Organisations have been reduced for long, they have lost high number of staff. For this reason, they give priority to those struggling with long-term use of heroin. This means they can't attend to other category of drug-users."

Dame Carol Black stated that recovery takes more than just treatment. She placed a strong emphasis on housing and employment. She applauded the government's effort in funding a pilot on the housing and employment needs of long-term drug users, however, she stated the need for more effort in this regard.

5.5 Phase two of Professor Dame Carol Black's report

The second part of Dame Black's findings was published on the 8th of July 2021. This second part explains why improvement is necessary, and suggests the kind of improvement that is needed to help with drug treatment, recovery, and prevention; the kind of improvements that will help people recover and turn their lives around.

Again, I will provide a summary of the report as well as her recommendations, but the full report is available on the UK's government website.

Her recommendations are as follows:

5.6 Diverting more offenders into treatment and recovery services

According to Dame Black's recommendations, a lot of people are "cycling in and out of prison, without achieving rehabilitation or recovery," and "The recent sentencing white paper committed to greater use of police diversions and community sentences with treatment as an alternative to custody." Additionally, she called for extra funding to be put towards building more treatment centres so that more people can be provided with adequate treatment and support.

5.7 The improvement of prisoners treatment experience in and out of prison

The Ministry of Justice, the Department for Health and Social Care and the NHS should work together to ensure that prisoners are supported when attending their treatment appointments while in prison. Upon their release from prison, they should be given adequate support when getting an ID, a bank account, and they should be able to claim benefits from the day of their release. Those with a dependence on drugs should be able to continue with their drug treatment after release.

5.8 Employment support

As Dame Black stated in the first part of her report, it takes more than treatment to aid recovery for someone who is battling drug addiction. She recommended that employment is a very important component of recovery. Employment helps the drug-user to achieve financial stability and to be positively pre-occupied. Employment support should be integrated within treatment centres. This action has been found to have yielded positive results through the deployment of the Individual Placement and Support (IPS) approach across seven local authorities. She suggested that the IPS model should be facilitated across all treatment centres in England.

The IPS model helps those struggling with severe mental health challenges get into employment. Under this approach, support is individualised to each person. Through this personalised support model, people are helped to get into paid employment that is suitable for them, Additionally, both the employee and the employer are supported

5.9 Housing

Drug dependence can both be a cause and consequence of homelessness. According to the Ministry of Housing, Communities and Local Government (MHCLG), almost two-thirds of rough sleepers struggle with drug or alcohol addiction. In addition to this, Public Health England (PHE)'s drug treatment data shows that one-fifth of adults who started treatment between 2019 and 2020 reported that they had housing problems, as well as one-third of people who are in treatment for opiates. Since it's an established fact that there is a strong link between homelessness and drug addiction, it is essential for housing assessments to be included during treatment and recovery. Fortunately, additional funding has been given to the MHCLG and the Department of Health and Social Care (DHSC) to improve treatment services.

Dame Black recommended that the appropriate government institutions need to plan more residential detoxification and rehabilitation centres across the country.
She also stated that more research should go into what works when tackling drug use, supply, treatment, and recovery. The government should also encourage and reward pharmaceutical research. Another recommendation was that the teaching of tobacco, alcohol, prescriptions, medicine, and illicit drugs must become part of school curriculum. Dame Black states that schoolteachers should be trained to deliver this knowledge effectively. Jobcentre Plus should also be given the power to provide outreach support to drug-users with complex needs, especially those within treatment centres.

Chapter 6
The old way the major way out

Going by Professor Dame Carol Black's findings, the country is in urgent need of relevant, innovative, and radical intervention. However, is the 19th century Police Court Mission still relevant and applicable? My three-year research led to a profound discovery which will open this chapter.

In 1877, George Nelson, the first police court missionary, gave a recommendation around a year after his assumption into this role. His first year in this position had given him the opportunity to gain a clearer understanding of the situation.

Nelson, who was appointed the first London police court missionary in August 1876, stated in his first report to the CETS in 1877, that those who were addicted to alcohol and brought before the court for alcohol-related offences should be placed "under medical care" instead of being sent to prison (CET Chronicle, 1877).

Coincidentally, more than a century later, the United Kingdom has found herself back in almost the same situation. In phase two of Professor Dame Carol Black's independent review, she also made a strikingly similar recommendation to that of George Nelson 142 years earlier!

Professor Dame Carol Black stated, as part of her recommendations, "Too many drug users are cycling in and out of prison. Rarely are prison sentences a restorative experience" (same stand as court missionaries). She went further to say, "Diversions from prison, and meaningful aftercare, have both been severely diminished and this trend must be reversed to break the costly cycle of addiction and offending." She suggested that "The recent sentencing white paper committed to greater use of police diversions and community sentences with treatment as an alternative to custody."

George Nelson's recommendation was taken on board and executed. The execution of his recommendation led to an overwhelmingly positive outcome: "This recommendation that institutionalised care would be the wisest course is one that, years later, the LPCM would implement with their 'inebriates' homes.'" (Porter, 1927)

The CETS responded to George Nelson's recommendation by establishing inebriates' homes. As I stated in Chapter 4, these were not just projects, they were residential abodes where the vulnerable found a family in the staff and volunteers who managed these homes. Court missionaries intentionally named these projects *homes* because they made them possess the same family ambiance as any other regular biological family home. A place where love and affection were shared with the residents. Of course, the outcome of these homes were the success stories from Chapter 4, of transformation shared by residents who used these homes. True love truly heals the world!

The response of the CETS to George Nelson's recommendation was a game changer. Will the government execute Professor Dame Carol Black's recommendation?

6.1 Central government response

Recommendations from over a hundred years ago have found their way back to the forefront as part of major solutions in the 21st century. The same issue, a different timeframe, and different people, but the same suggested solutions.

I want to give a brief analysis on the government's response to Prof. Dame Carol Black's recommendation. It has loads of positives, however, I'd like to call the government's attention to the lessons learnt from history over a hundred years ago, so that the same mistakes made then will not repeat themselves now.

I have highlighted a summary of the government's response below. Full details of the response are covered in a document called *From harm to hope: a 10 year drugs plan to cut crime and save lives* and is available on the UK's government website.

The government split their proposed strategy into three categories.

6.2 Breaking the drug chain supply

This plan illustrates how the government plans to crack down on organised crime groups, protect our prisons from drug use and supply, secure our borders, and deal with county lines.

6.3 Delivering a world-class treatment and recovery system

This intervention contains the government's plan to treat addiction as a chronic health condition, tackle the stigma linked to addiction, save lives, and break the cycle of crime linked to addiction. Furthermore, the intervention also contains a plan to rebuild the workforce's attitude towards the physical and mental health of people suffering with addiction, improve service integration, provide accommodation alongside treatment, and keep prisoners engaged in treatment after their release from prison.

6.4 Achieve generational shift in demand for drugs

The government seeks to change the societal attitude surrounding the perceived acceptability of illegal drug use. To achieve this intervention, the plan is to use evidence-based research, introduce tougher consequences for users and dealers of drugs, deploy school-based prevention methods where school pupils are taught the dangers of drug and alcohol use, and provide support for young people and families who are most at risk of substance misuse.

The government have also revealed how they plan to achieve these goals. The summary is as follows:

- By ensuring that almost half of people experiencing homelessness have a drug support system.

- Since 2021, the government has budgeted £148 million towards crime reduction and the protection of people from harm caused by illegal drugs. More than half of this new budget will be put towards treatment and recovery services.

- The expansion of Project ADDER (addiction, disruption, diversion, enforcement and recovery). According to the government website, this programme "focuses on coordinated law enforcement activity, alongside expanded diversionary programmes (such as Out of Court Disposal orders), using the criminal justice system to divert people away from offending." This £59 million programme was expected to run from 2020 to 2023 but has recently been extended for another two years.

- That there is an allocation of £6.1 million to extend the IPS programme across England. This announcement was made in May 2021 by the Department for Work and Pensions (DWP).

- That an additional £700,000 has been made into His Majesty's Prison and Probation Service for ten health and justice partnership coordinators to work closely with health and substance misuse partners locally. Their main aim will be to improve the continuity of care from custody to release.

- That the Ministry of Justice (MoJ) is budgeting £1.3 million to deliver telemedicine in 86 prisons. This will help to establish contact and relationships between prisoners and treatment providers in the community. The plan is that these relationships will allow prisoners to continue their treatment after their release from prison.

- To identify and deal with those involved in crime and drug misuse. The government is planning on executing and increasing the use of drug testing on arrests in several police forces across England and Wales.

- There is a roundtable discussion planned by the Home Office with major stakeholders, especially the Ministry of Justice, the Department of Health and Social Care, policing, and other drug intervention experts. The discussion will focus on understanding innovative and effective ways to reduce the demand and use of illegal drugs. Part of this discussion will also include mapping out clear and meaningful consequences for those who do misuse drugs. Consequences will include fines, community service, referrals to drug treatment programmes and drug awareness courses.

- The government website further states that "As part of this we will learn from, strengthen and develop the meaningful consequences being developed by some forces, including those such as Thames Valley and Durham, to most effectively deal with those who use illegal drugs and those who might be tempted to do so."

- There is a plan for a summit to be held with other relevant stakeholders including employers, educators, law enforcement and health organisations. This summit will look at gaining a deeper understanding on how to tackle illicit drug use as well as to help users stop using drugs.

6.5 Analysis of this response.

In fairness, a lot of these interventions are commendable. Personally, I am excited at the prospect of the school-based prevention and knowledge programme. Teaching primary school aged children about the danger of drugs and alcohol is a very effective way of achieving prevention. I mentioned in Chapter 3, while writing about Frederic Rainer, about how the right education can positively influence someone's thoughts, reactions, and attitude in society. I believe that Rainer's education at a national school must have played a huge part in his contribution to society. Achieving a generational shift isn't just about building a new generation, but strengthening the values that contributed to the social stability of the past. The same values that were dispensed by national schools should be revisited and reinstated.

My concern is that even though the strategy is a ten-year strategy, the fundamental funding, and programmes necessary to execute the plans are very short-term. Some of them are less than the ten-year period.

For example, plan number 3 talks about expanding Project ADDER, which has been reported to have recorded some level of success. Project ADDER is an "expanded diversionary programmes (such as Out of Court Disposal orders), using the criminal justice system to divert people away from offending."

Project ADDER has reportedly achieved tremendous results in less than three years, this includes the disruption of 2,749 organised crime gangs, the seizing of £9.8m in cash, making 27,876 drug possession charges and 3,808 drug trafficking charges.

According to the West Yorkshire Police website, in Wakefield, £12.8m worth of drugs have been seized in the past two years through Project ADDER. This is just one achievement out of many that has been made in Wakefield alone.

However, Project ADDER is now scheduled to end in March 2025. Bear in mind that this is a ten-year strategy, but in less than five years one of the strategies will no longer exist despite its effectiveness.

One important factor for any government intervention is that government work is based on priority. The priority of the government is heavily dependent on the prevailing socio-economic challenges of the time. This means, a major social challenge today might receive less government attention in the future if another urgent social challenge emerges. This would mean that funding could shift towards new challenges. Plans number 2 through 6 have a financial commitment, but the sustainability of these programmes and any associated funding is a great concern.

Also, an intervention like IPS, according to Professor Dame Carol Black's recommendation, has worked successfully in seven local authorities in England. Such interventions should be sustained on a long-term basis because of their impact. However, only £6.1m has been budgeted for it. What happens after these funds run out? Will this intervention continue even when priorities change?

Chapter 7
Emerging rescue mission

Josh MacAlister's independent review on children's social care (which I wrote about in Chapter 4) and Professor Dame Carol Black's review (which I wrote about in the last two chapters) point to one fact: we need another rescue mission to support and collaborate with the government. Like the 19th century rescue mission, key players must once again rise to the task. Missionaries and magistrates were the key players of the 19th century. Every level of government as well as churches and Christian organisations have been identified as key players of the 21st century rescue mission.

I strongly believe for example, that interventions like 'Levelling Up' should engage the involvement of local Churches and Christian Organisations. According to Government website (gov.uk, 2022) *"Levelling up is a mission to challenge, and change, that unfairness. Levelling up means giving everyone the opportunity to flourish. It means people everywhere living longer and more fulfilling lives, and benefiting from sustained rises in living standards and well-being".* Part of the next phase and focus of the project is to restore a sense of the local communities, local pride and belonging in places where these have been lost. The project also seeks to empower local leaders and communities especially in communities lacking local agency.

Local churches and Christian Organisations fit in perfectly to this mission. With the provision of funding, local churches will serve the community with similar passion, love, enthusiasm and commitment as the court missionaries. Our Organisation (Shine Development Concept CIC) and

New Covenant Church in Northampton with the support of other 3rd sector Organisations, the University of Northampton, and local businesses, we provided winter night shelter till covid-19 hit. Northampton Borough Council provided night shelter for men and we provided for women. The synergy provided necessary support for the homeless community in Northampton.

According to Cassady (2001), "This was the foundation of the working relationship between the church and police courts because it appeared both institutions were fighting a common cause."

True collaboration is unavoidable if we want to experience true social transformation. The recommendations and responses from both independent reviews point in this direction.

There are four major reasons why this collaboration is needed:

Firstly, the staff shortage and heavy workload. Professor Dame Carol Black, in her findings, pointed out a significant shortage of staff and experts. According to her, "Local authorities normally work with the NHS Trust and not-for-profit organisations to provide treatment. However, because the funding of both NHS Trusts and not-for-profit organisations has been reduced for a long time, they have lost a high number of staff. For this reason, they give priority to those struggling with long-term use of heroin." This means they can't attend to other categories of drug-users. This is a major obstacle; however, it is important to note that this problem made the London police courts open their doors to collaboration with the Church of England Temperance Society back in the 18th century.

Auerbach (2015) says, "Since their formal establishment in 1792, these courts had also provided advice, interpersonal conflict resolution, and even informal charity, but their ability to do so had been severely limited by the ever-increasing demands to process summons and charges, by limited financial resources, and by a critical shortage of personnel."

To reiterate, it was the huge workload, funding cuts and a shortage of staff that made London police courts open their doors for the Church in the 18th century. These problems are not new. The solution deployed then is also relevant now. The doors must be open to form sustainable partnerships with the Church and Christian organisations to tackle drug use and homelessness across the board.

The second reason is that it would save costs. Financially, the government would spend less, and reasonable financial investment would still be made in the hands of government agencies. At this point, I need to remind you that even with little resources, the early court missionaries made an undeniable impact.

"The Magistrates as a body began to notice the striking effects produced by the Missionaries, even under the very limited opportunities they had before 1887. This led to a serious questioning of the real value of the system of fines and imprisonment. Was it remedial? No, for in nine cases out of ten the offender came out of prison worse, or at all events no better, than he went in." (Porter, 1927)

Churches and Christian organisations have an emotional connection to the communities that they are a part of, and only want the best for these communities. Most of the time, they have either direct or mutual contact with almost everyone, and their personal affiliation is remarkable. This is extremely different from having a public servant — a public servant who lived and grew up elsewhere — handle an official responsibility in an environment that they are not affiliated with. In situations such as these, the work is handled from an official perspective only. Personal connection is likely not involved.

I want to share a particular experience highlighted in the CETS report of 1885. A woman came to one of the early court missionaries, Batchelor, for assistance. This is because both hers and her husband's drinking habit had cost them their house. According to Batchelor, the woman said they were "in a wretched condition ... scarcely anything on her back!" Batchelor not only gave her some money from his personal funds, but he also used his influence to get the woman a job. Batchelor reported that at the time of compiling his report in 1885, the woman was still in employment, and she had received a good character commendation from her employer!

7.1 Viable partnership examples

The first shelter (which I mentioned earlier in this chapter) we managed at Shine Development Concept CIC cost us less than £30,000, and this was during winter. The shelter was carried out in partnership with New Covenant Church, Northampton. The shelter was located inside the Church building. The project supported over 300 people who were experiencing homelessness during the 100 nights between December and March. We offered hot meals every night, laundry service, showers, and other means of caring for their personal hygiene as well as free, warm sleeping space. Staff from Northampton Borough Council came over to support eligible users into temporary accommodation. The Northampton General Hospital also donated free medical equipment, with which medical professionals checked shelter users' temperature and blood pressure every Friday. All for free. The users of the shelter didn't have to pay a penny. We only had to pay a few key staff members and purchase essential resources, but we were able to draw a huge pool of volunteers from churches and the wider community who invested their time, resources, and energy into this great cause.

In Derbyshire, up until Covid-19, the Derby City mission collaborated with churches across Derby City and Derbyshire to house people who were battling homelessness every winter. This project ended up saving a lot of money for the local government.

These are all valuable examples of what the government would get from a partnership with churches and Christian organisations.

A collaboration between the government and the Church would answer the problem and social challenge that the UK, and countries across the globe, are currently experiencing. Christians are guided by the same ethics everywhere around the world. This collaboration is cost-effective and reflects value for money.

Thirdly, there is a big trust issue between communities and the system. Underserved communities find it difficult to engage with government services, this is likely due to failures and let-downs that they have experienced in the past.

This distrust goes back for over a hundred years. As a matter of fact, one of the reasons why the early court missionaries recorded so much success was because the local community did not associate them with the police or any official government system (Porter, 1927).

This distrust still exists. This fact has become clear to me throughout my decade of work experience with both voluntary and public sector organisations. I must sincerely commend the government's effort in aiming to make amends. Part of the Equality Act of 2010 is one of those commendable efforts. Besides that, the government is doing a lot in terms of addressing health inequalities and wider determinants. However, a partnership with the Church and

Christian charities will augment government efforts and yield more productive results. Churches and Christian charities are already doing a lot. I gave an example earlier of the shelter that Shine Development Concept CIC managed in Northampton all because the New Covenant Church opened their doors for those battling homelessness during the coldest months of winter.

Fourthly, the Church and Christian organisations stand tall as a force of true sacrificial love and divine compassion. As evidenced in previous chapters, this is necessary for successful community development. Early magistrates couldn't find words to describe this sacrificial love and divine compassion. The sacrifice was mind-blowing, some called it "kind sympathy." In the words of an early magistrate, John Dickinson, and his colleague Frederic Meade, "the work in such a Court as Thames, and in such a poor and densely populated district as this, must necessarily be very heavy, but your energy, attention, and kindly sympathy have never failed. Your work is a great one, helping the weak and tempted, comforting the miserable and hopeless, and striving to rescue the forlorn and vicious." (CETS Annual Report, 1890)

This attribute sets the Church and Christian organisations apart. This was the secret behind the early 19th century court missionaries who were stirring change. It is intrinsic and divine. This divine compassion and sacrificial love are born in every Christian who has experienced genuine salvation through Jesus Christ. There is no other way to explain it than that.

"The Police Court Mission was founded in the overcoming power of the living Christ." (Porter, 1927)

That is just the simple way to put it. This "overcoming power of the living Christ" expresses itself through divine compassion and sacrificial love that overlooks the shortcomings of people and society.

The Christian expression of faith has an inbuilt tenacity when it comes to loving the vulnerable. This expression of love is compelling and melts the heart of the recipient.

Finally, in this collaboration and coproduction, training should be provided for churches and Christian organisations. This will provide them with the best possible opportunity to execute the administrative component of the work efficiently and within legal framework. Of course, as I have stated earlier in this chapter, a consistent and considerable amount of funding must be invested into this collaboration by the government, and in the long run, it will help the government save money.

7.2 Examples of a few existing Christian charities

The Church of England is still well known for the passion it has for its communities. The Redeemed Christian Church of God (RCCG) is another thriving Pentecostal Church in the United Kingdom with a huge drive for social action and community development. One of the strengths of the Church is its numbers, The Redeemed Christian Church of God has over 800 branches across the United Kingdom and the Church is present in over 190 countries across the world. The Church has a thriving CSR (Corporate Social Responsibility) team that supports all branches with their social action endeavors. Branches of the RCCG tackle different social challenges within their individual communities such as food and fuel poverty, child hunger, supporting shelters for the homeless.

Jesus House for All Nations in Brent Cross London runs a project called "Christmas lunch on Jesus". This project has distributed well over 20000 food hampers during Christmas since its inception. The idea behind it is to deliver quality food hampers to those in need and their families during Christmas. Not only that, but the Church also volunteered her building during covid-19 as a vaccination Centre. King Charles (then Prince Charles) paid a courtesy visit to the Centre during this period.

There are other Christian charities doing amazing work across the United Kingdom, and I will name a few and what they do. Detailed information about them can also be found online.

Carpenters Arm, Loughborough. They provide amazing Christian residential support for drug recovery and rehabilitation. I visited the project in 2019, and the senior staff I spoke to during my visit was actually someone who had once been given support from the charity. He had successfully evolved from being a volunteer junior member staff to becoming a senior member of staff in the same organisation where he was once a beneficiary. (www.carpenters-arms.org)

Derby City Mission is another Christian charity that supports people facing homelessness. Part of their work is to partner with churches across different communities during winter to use their church buildings as homeless shelters for those battling homelessness. (www.derbycitymission.org.uk)

Freedom Community Project is a Christian charity based in Bolsover, Derbyshire and branches across both Derbyshire and Nottinghamshire. They provide free benefit advice and support, debt advice and support, free community cafes, a free food bank and more. (www.freedom.charity)

Christian Against Poverty is another charity that offers tremendous support in financial literacy and helps people make educated financial decisions. (www.capuk.org)

Compassion UK is an international children's charity that was founded in 1952. Compassion believes its an injustice that 356 million children worldwide live in extreme poverty. Therefore, they believe as a Christian organisation that they have a biblical call to care for the poor and love their neighbour. That's why they work in partnership with local churches to release children from poverty, in Jesus' name. Their work spans across 29 countries, and they're currently partnering with 8,500 local churches within communities experiencing poverty. Their passion is to give children and young people the opportunity to thrive and reach their God-given potential now and in the future. (www.compassionuk.org)

Wonderful Way CIC is another Christian social enterprise with a strong vision to support families and individuals living in poverty and help them get back on their feet through their poverty alleviation and intervention programmes. Wonderful Way CIC provides both relevant subsistence and long-term recovery support through key practical services to deprived communities across the United Kingdom. Their services include free money management support workshops, a food bank and toiletries support, financial management masterclasses, a mini money management camp for KS1 & KS2 pupils, and a freshers financial bootcamp for ages 16+. (www.wonderfulwaycic.com)

The New Covenant Church Northampton worked in collaboration with Shine Development Concept CIC to facilitate the first winter shelter in Northampton. They co-produced the project with members of the public, third sector volunteers and residents of the county. The Church opens its doors for 100 nights throughout the cold winter months for people battling homelessness in Northampton. Users of this shelter can gain access to the shelter through either personal or professional referral. This made the facility flexible and accessible to anyone. (www.newcovenantchurch.org.uk)

Shine Development Concept CIC is a Christian community interest company (CIC) who support people experiencing hardship. They place priority on families that have under-age children. Their food bank provides both regular English food items as well as African, Caribbean, and Asian food items to nonEU immigrants. Before Covid-19, they collaborated with a local church in Northampton to provide free shelter every winter to people struggling with homelessness.

The organisation also partners with a major financial institution in the UK to provide mentorship for youths from black communities with the aim of improving their employability skills and support them in achieving their career goals. Shine CIC runs a community café where Nigerian snacks and breakfast foods are served along with free fruit. The café serves as a safe space for ethnic minority communities to form relationships. It tackles social isolation and addresses food poverty and health inequalities in black communities in Northampton. At the Café, food is served for free donations, prevention and management of health challenges peculiar to black communities is also addressed by health professionals. People who come to the café also gain free access to the New Covenant Church's community gym in the same building. (www.shinecic.org.uk)

These are just a few examples out of many similar initiatives offered by Churches, and Christian Organisations in the United Kingdom. It is evident that the nation, and of course, the world at large is in dire need of another rescue mission. Missionaries and the magistrates formed this rescue in the 19th century, but a similar collaboration must occur, and the time is now! There are more than enough potential partners for the government to executive social transformation and development in the UK.

Chapter 8
Starting a new community organisation?

While we have numerous Churches and Christian charities doing great work around the country, there's still a need for similar organisations within our communities. There are still social gaps that require urgent attention.

An analysis by Prof. Dame Carol Black has identified a few reasons behind drug use and supply. If we want to successfully tackle addiction, those reasons must be addressed. We must also provide solutions to help solve the problem, a few of these are as follows:

- Tackling poverty of all forms, including food poverty, child poverty and deprivation

- Addressing the lack of employability skills throughout the nation

- Providing English language lessons for non-English speaking immigrants

- Supporting ex-offenders from the first day of their release

- Establishing shelters for the homeless, and providing support with finding temporary accommodation

- More inpatient drug rehabilitation centres

- Providing support for children in care and children leaving care

- Providing awareness to children, young people and vulnerable adults on the importance of online safety

- Supporting children who are facing school exclusion

- Offering therapy for spouses and immediate family members of people who suffer from addiction

- Raising awareness of county lines for parents and young people

If you are a Church or a Christian who is willing to tackle any of the gaps listed above, or if you want to start or grow your own idea, you can reach out to your local Community Development Officer for advice. Every local authority has one, so if you can't find yours, you can either phone the council to ask or check online to see if you can find their contact details there.

Your local Community Development Officer supports communities or individuals who are working towards social change. They are an extremely strong link between communities and community groups who provide relevant services to those in need. A huge chunk of their work is to ensure that the quality of life in their community is constantly improving.

Community Development Officers are your first point of contact. They will advise you on what you need to know and do. They will connect you with those in the community that need your service, and they are very helpful.

Another critical point of contact for help in facilitating your community project is your community foundation. Almost every council has a community foundation. For example, Northamptonshire has Northamptonshire Community Foundation. They specialise in giving you advice regarding the funding of your project. They hold different kind of grants for different categories of projects. If you tell them which project you have in mind, they will advise you on the best option of grants and funding that would suit your project.

Another relevant contact is the incorporated Voluntary, Community, and Social Enterprise Organisations (VCSE). They are voluntary or charitable organisations that serve the community. Almost all counties in England would have one of these. You can contact them for advice, or for help with linking you up to other community organisations in your area.

Chapter 9
The unique love story

Some called it 'kind sympathy,' others called it 'unusual love.' But whatever it was called was not the main issue, what mattered the most was the effect the Church of England Temperance Society had on the country through the police court missionaries.

Offenders ought to be punished. Relatively, the magistrates weren't wrong in handing out judgment to those who committed alcohol-related crimes. However, punishment didn't save the offender. Those sentenced, according to J. Hasloch Porter, came out of prison worse. Offenders continued drowning in their own bad habits.

The Church saw a different picture and offered a different solution. They offered what they had received, unusual compassion, mercy, and love from God through Jesus Christ. A Christian holds mercy and love in high esteem because that was what saved him/her from sin. Sin hurts the world, but genuine love saves the world.

That is why the Church came on the scene and provided the condemned with mercy and love. The result was obvious, It saved the nation.

The United Kingdom is God's love story through Jesus Christ. The probation story of the United Kingdom is one which weighs the subject of sin, condemnation and judgment against love and mercy that brings redemption. The Church didn't judge those who were brought to court, because Jesus Christ didn't judge the world when He came to the earth over 2000 years ago to save it. What He did was offer a rare type of love that leads to redemption. The very same way the love showed by the court missionaries saved offenders who were condemned.

"For God did not send His Son into the world to condemn the world, but that the world through Him might be saved." **(John 3:17 NKJV)**

The United Kingdom probation story is an illustration of God's redemptive love. No sin of man outweighs God's love through Jesus Christ. This love gives a brand-new start, opens another chapter of life filled with fulfilment and hope in Jesus Christ. Those who received the love of the police court missionaries had their lives changed. No man is excluded from this love that heals and brings change. His arms are still wide open, and the love is as pure and available now as it was back then.

References

Auerbach, S. (2015). "Beyond the Pale of Mercy": Victorian Penal Culture, Police Court Missionaries, and the Origins of Probation in England

Cassady, S. (2001). Frederic Rainer: The Founder Of Probation? Probation Journal, 48(4), 287–289. https://doi.org/10.1177/026455050104800406

CETS Annual Report 1885

CETS Annual Report 1889, 1890 and 1891

CETS Annual Report 1902

CETS Annual Report 1903

2nd Corinthians 5:16a. Holy Bible. The Passion Translation.

Crisis (2023) Ending Homelessness. Available at

https://www.crisis.org.uk/ending-homelessness/about-homelessness/. Last accessed on the 1st of June 2023

Government Website (2022) Levelling up the United Kingdom. Available at https://www.gov.uk/government/publications/levelling-up-the-united-kingdom. Last accessed on the 3rd of February 2024.

Jennings P., (2012), "Policing Drunkenness in England and Wales from the Late Eighteenth Century to the First World War," Social History of Alcohol and Drugs

John 3:17, Holy Bible. New King James Version

Larking D., (2022) Robert Peels hidden prayer. Available at https://betweentwocities.com/2017/02/17/sir-robert-peels-hidden-prayer/. Last accessed on the 3rd of August 2023

McWilliams, W., (1983) 'The Mission to the English Police Courts 1876-1936', in Howard Journal 22, pp.l29-147

Parliament Library (2022), Children Social Care Independent Review. Available at https://lordslibrary.parliament.uk/independent-review-of-childrens-social-care/#:~:text=It%20recommended%20the%20development%20of,by%20a%20national%20practice%20group. Last accessed in the June 2023

Parliament Website (2023) Metropolitan Police. Available at https://www.parliament.uk/about/living-heritage/transformingsociety/laworder/policeprisons/overview/metropolitanpolice/. Last accessed on the 3rd of February 2024

"Police-Court Work," Church of England Temperance Chronicle (hereafter CET Chronicle), September 1, 1877, 147 (Lambeth Palace Archives)

Porter, J.H., (1927) Inasmuch: The Story of the Police Court Mission. (London: Williams & Norgate)

Rainer Foundation Archive, Nottingham Gallery of Justice

Shelter (2023) What causes homelessness. Available at https://england.shelter.org.uk/support_us/campaigns/what_causes_homelessness#:~:text=Discrimination%20and%20inequality,at%20greater%20risk%20of%20homelessness. Last accessed on the 22nd of August 2023

UK Government Website (2021) Harm to Hope: A 10 year drugs plan to cut crime and save lives. (https://www.gov.uk/government/publications/from-harm-to-hope-a-10-year-drugs-plan-to-cut-crime-and-save-lives/from-harm-to-hope-a-10-year-drugs-plan-to-cut-crime-and-save-lives. Last accessed April 2023

UK Government Website (2022) Independent Review of drugs by Professor Dame Carol Black https://www.gov.uk/government/collections/independent-review-of-drugs-by-professor-dame-carol-black. Last accessed June 2023

West Yorkshire Police (2023) Project ADDER dismantling criminal gangs dealing drugs in Wakefield district https://www.westyorkshire.police.uk/news-appeals/project-adder-dismantling-criminal-gangs-dealing-drugs-wakefield-district. Last accessed in August 2023.

https://www.actionforchildren.org.uk/blog/

www.rccguk.church

www.carpenters-arms.org

www.derbycitymission.org.uk

www.freedom.charity

www.capuk.org

www.compassionuk.org

www.wonderfulwaycic.com

www.newcovenantchurch.org.uk

www.shinecic.org.uk

Profile

Ayodeji (Ayo) Ogunbuyide has over ten years experience working with underserved and marginalised communities in the UK. This experience has enabled him to gain first hand insight into the troubles of these communities. He has co-produced some innovative and sustainable interventions in tackling food poverty, homelessness, health inequalities, financial exclusion, marginalisation, and has given free mentorship to young people from ethnic minority communities.

Apart from his vast track record of work within the UK's public service and third sector, Ayo was the pioneer Chair for Northamptonshire Black Communities Together. This is a collection of around 28 black community groups, charities, and organisations across Northamptonshire.

Ayo runs a UK registered Christian Community-Interest-Company called Shine Development Concept CIC with his wife. Over the last decade, Shine Development Concept CIC has provided over 10,000 free food parcels for families with no/low-income, families where children rely on free school meals, families in need, ex-offenders, people battling homelessness and people with severe health conditions. The organisation runs a food bank that supports immigrants with 'no recourse to public funds' Immigration status. The foodbank provides traditional African, Asian and Caribbean food items.

Shine Development Concept CIC partners with a leading financial institution in the UK to provide mentorship to young black people in the UK. From 2017 up until Covid-

19 struck in 2020, Shine Development Concept CIC partnered with New Covenant Church in Northampton and other strategic stakeholders within the public, private and third sector to facilitate yearly free winter night shelter for people battling homelessness and rough sleeping. Over 300 people were supported with free warm sleeping spaces, free hot meals, free laundry and personal hygiene facilities, and support in finding temporary accommodation.

Ayo is a trained Project Manager and bagged his Masters degree from the University of Northampton in Youth and Community Leadership. He is married to Oluwaseun, and together they have two lovely children named Mofi and Sam. With his wife, he pastors a growing Church with The Redeemed Christian Church of God in the United Kingdom.

Milton Keynes UK
Ingram Content Group UK Ltd.
UKHW020311101124
450803UK00006BA/100